SYMPOSIUM IN MEMORY OF KEI MORI

STUDIES IN ECONOMIC DYNAMICS

SYMPOSIUM IN MEMORY OF KEI MORI

STUDIES IN ECONOMIC DYNAMICS

Tokyo
26 April 1993

Editor

Lawrence R. Klein
University of Pennsylvania

World Scientific
Singapore • New Jersey • London • Hong Kong

Published by

World Scientific Publishing Co. Pte. Ltd.

5 Toh Tuck Link, Singapore 596224

USA office: 27 Warren Street, Suite 401-402, Hackensack, NJ 07601

UK office: 57 Shelton Street, Covent Garden, London WC2H 9HE

Library of Congress Cataloging-in-Publication Data

Klein, Lawrence Robert.

Symposium in memory of Kei Mori: studies in economic dynamics / editor, Lawrence R. Klein.

p. cm.

Includes bibliographical references.

ISBN-13 978-981-02-2054-9 -- ISBN-10 981-02-2054-5

1. Mori, Kei, 1932–1990 -- Contributions in economics -- Congresses. 2. Economists -- Japan -- Congresses. 3. Econometrics -- Congresses. 4. Statics and dynamics (Social sciences) -- Congresses. I. Title.

HB126.J4M675 1995

330.1--dc20 95-11735

CIP

British Library Cataloguing-in-Publication Data

A catalogue record for this book is available from the British Library.

Dedicated to Yoko Mori

CONTENTS

PREFACE

Dr. Kei Mori followed two interesting paths during his professional career, which was cut short by an untimely death at age 57. His degrees were all in Economics, at Keio University, Tokyo, Japan. He completed a Bachelor's degree in 1955, a Master's in 1958, and Doctorate in 1968. His faculty appointments, however were in the Faculty of Technology at Keio, in the Department of Administration Engineering.

He pursued an engineering career during the 1980s with an interest in sunlight supply to sheltered and shaded places (e.g. in buildings) transmitted through optical fiber systems. His death occurred on February 15, 1990.

Prior to his creative work in technology during the final decade of his life, he made significant contributions to Economics during the 1960s and 1970s. An economic symposium in his memory was organized in Tokyo in 1993, and the present volume reports on the presentations made on that occasion. A number of Kei Mori's Japanese colleagues attended that symposium to present papers that were related to his fields of special interest, to comment on the papers, or to listen to the papers under discussion.

For more than twenty years, I interacted in economic studies with Kei Mori and was his friend in many inter-related family or other personal events ever since we first met in 1968, in Philadelphia.

Kei Mori's work in Economics followed three lines of development that interested me a great deal. In the first place, he made contributions to dynamic macroeconomics through the construction and analysis of statistical models. This work intersected with my own interests and form the basis for the contents of the present volume. When he arrived on the scene at the University of Pennsylvania, we were deeply involved with constructing and using the various vintages of the Wharton Econometric Models, and he made important contributions to those ongoing endeavors. All during this period, I hosted many visitors from Japan in the field of econometrics, and Kei Mori fitted neatly into the group of Americans and visitors who were actively engaged in exciting new developments. Dr. Mori's thesis work at Keio was directly in line with Pennsylvania econometrics, and he certainly added important content to our work. The evaluation of characteristic roots (eigenvalues) of large scale dynamic systems and the design of stabilization policy were specific problems where Kei Mori's contributions were very significant.

Dr. Mori arrived at Pennsylvania during the waning years of the Vietnam War, when we were studying the impact of possible settlement with demobilization, conversion, and related fiscal changes for the US government.

At the end of the Second World War and the Korean War, predecessor models of the Wharton Models were used with great success in analyzing the consequences of settlement of the conflicts. It was only natural that we were engaged, in the Wharton group, in making similar analyses of the ending of the War in Vietnam. I collaborated with Kei Mori in a study prepared for the Arms Control and Disarmament Agency on the macro dynamic patterns of settlement in Vietnam. We argued, with the help of the Wharton Model, that a peace settlement would be advantageous for the US economy.

That was not the last of collaborative work that I undertook with Kei Mori on the economics of defense spending for he sent his student and colleague, Hiroyuki Kosaka, also of Keio University, to Pennsylvania for post doctoral research on the dynamics of the "Arms Race" between the two superpowers — USA and USSR — each supported by allied nations, NATO and WTO (Warsaw Treaty Organization). Dr. Kosaka came to Philadelphia with action–reaction models of the Richardson type, and we ultimately simulated this kind of system with the international LINK model, then centered at the Economics Department of the University of Pennsylvania. Dr. Kosaka is a participating author in the present volume.

The third line of economics-related research activity undertaken by Kei Mori was in the delivery and use of quantitative information in large-scale econometric systems. The early years of Project LINK, a model of the international transmission mechanism among leading economies of the world, took place over the period when Kei Mori was at Pennsylvania. The Project was designed to bring model builders from all over the world together to achieve mutually consistent operation of the international trading mechanism.

Project LINK was conceived at a time when efficient computing for econometrics was in its infancy, but Kei Mori's ideas were far ahead of others in this respect, undoubtedly related to his technical engineering bent. We had great trouble, in LINK, collecting information (data) from worldwide points in timely fashion for quick response to changing global economic situations. Kei Mori conceived plans for satellite transmission of updated data bases from all the far flung LINK participants via available computer network systems. For years, after he had departed from Pennsylvania, we corresponded and often met to discuss the data collection–transmission problem in fast and reliable machine-readable form. We were able to do such things one decade or more after Kei Mori had worked out the conceptual scheme.

One of our last face-to-face encounters took place when he was near Philadelphia in connection with advising Japanese universities on a communications/computing network system.

In recognition of his contributions to Economics, some of his friends or colleagues and I got together in Tokyo for the symposium presented in the present volume.

Lawrence R. Klein
November, 1994

CURRICULUM VITAE

late Dr. KEI MORI

BORN	:	November 20, 1932
DIED	:	February 15, 1990, left wife and two daughters
EDUCATION	:	
1955		BA in Economics, Keio University, Tokyo
1958		MA in Economics, Keio University, Tokyo
1968		Ph D. in Economics, Keio University, Tokyo
RESEARCH AND TEACHING EXPERIENCE	:	
1968–70		Research Associate, University of Pennsylvania (Wharton School), Philadelphia
1968		Assistant Professor, Department of Administration Engineering Faculty of Technology, Keio University
1969 (Summer)		Brookings Institution, Washington, DC
1973		Professor, Department of Administration Engineering, Faculty of Technology, Keio University
1981		Professor, Department of Administration Engineering, Faculty of Science and Technology, Keio University
BUSINESS EXPERIENCE	:	
1978		Founder of La Foret Engineering and Information Service Co., Ltd. for manufacturing the "Himawari" sunlight collecting/transmitting system.
1985		Chairman of the above-mentioned company

PUBLIC ACTIVITIES AND PROFESSIONAL AFFILIATIONS:

Project leader, Redevelopment of Roppongi-Akasaka for Center-City Tokyo (ARK Hills Project)

Chairman, Office Research on Building Information Technology in Japan (ORBIT)

Vice Chairman, Japan Institute for Macro-Engineering

Executive Director, Association of Computer Education for Private Universities in Japan

Trustee, Database Promotion Center of Japan

Trustee, Marine Biotechnology Research Society of Japan

Member, Research Committee for Designing Integrated Regional Information Systems for The Japan Association for Planning Administration

Member, Theoretical and Econometric Society of Japan

Member, Information Processing Society of Japan

Member, Japan Society for Aeronautical and Space Sciences

Member, Illuminating Engineering Institute of Japan

AWARDS:

The Himawari Building — the headquarters of La Foret Engineering and Information Service Co., Ltd. — installed with the "Sol-air Heat Recovery Type Heat Pump System," in addition to the Himawari sunlight collecting/transmitting system, both of which have been developed by Dr. Kei Mori, won a "most excellent" award from the Committee of Rational Utilization of Electricity in the Ministry of International Trade and Industry, Japanese Government in 1985.

Honorary Degree Doctor of Science from Carnegie Mellon University, 1990.

PUBLICATIONS:

Major Books

1. "Simulation analysis of growth and fluctuations in Japanese economy," in ed. Komiya, *Economic Growth of Postwar Japanese Economy* (Iwanami Publishing Company, 1963) (in Japanese).
2. "Optimal planning methods for econometric models to attain desired tradeoff between degrees of achievement of several objectives," in ed. Myoken, *Information Decisions and Control in Dynamic Economic Systems* (Bunshindo Publishing Company, 1978), with F. Yoda.
3. "Developing user-participated database in econometric models," in ed. Shishido, *Statistical Data Bank Systems* (North-Holland Publishing Company, 1988).

Major Articles on Economic Analysis

1. "Simulation analysis of Japanese economy," *Economic Analysis* (1960), pp. 1–7 (in Japanese).
2. "Simulation analysis for Japanese economy," in ed. Morishima, *New Methods for Economic Analysis* (Sobunsha, 1960), pp. 211–241 (in Japanese).
3. "Economic forecast and econometrics-predictive performance for the Japanese economy," *Ministry of International Trade and Industry Review*, vol. **10**, no. 3, pp. 24–45 (1962) (in Japanese).
4. "Quarterly economic models of the postwar Japanese economy and resonance effect of its interest rate policy," *Zeitschrift fur Gesamte Staatswissenschaft*, **122** Band, 4 Heft., pp. 616–685 (1963).
5. "Impact of disarmament on aggregate economic activity — An econometric analysis," *US Arms Control and Disarmament Agency (ACDA)*; E-156 (1970).
6. "Generalized eigenvalue problem of econometric model," *Econometrica*, vol. **39**, no. 4 (1971).
7. "Monte Carlo study of principal component two stage least square method," *Proceedings of Japanese Society of Economics and Econometrics*, pp. 57–69 (1971), with H. Kosaka (in Japanese).
8. "Econometric modeling system," *Proceedings of Information Processing*, pp. 349–350 (1977) (in Japanese).

9. "Design of economic database and econometric modeling system," *Hitotsubashi Ronso*, vol. **80**, pp. 158–184 (1978), with Y. Kurabayashi (in Japanese).

Main Articles on Sunlight Supply System

1. "A lighting system for supplying visible solar light with fiber-optic cables," *14th National Congress of the Illuminating Engineering Institute of Japan*, pp. 22–24 (April 3, 1981) (in Japanese).
2. "Automatic solar ray collection and transmission system," *The Japan Society of Mechanical Engineers, R & D Committee on Alternative Energy*, pp. 62–65 (February 5, 1982).
3. "An experimental system for an ecologically controlled environment," *Space Station Symposium of The Japan Society for Aeronautics and Space Sciences*, pp. 67–83 (June 27, 1983) (in Japanese).
4. "Value added solar ray supply system transmitted through optical fiber with automatic solar ray collection 'Himawari'," *The Technical Forum on Optical Technology Application System in City Area*, pp. 1–12 (March 1984).
5. "Visible solar-ray supply system for space station," *Acta Astronautica*, vol. **13**, no. 2, pp. 71–79 (1985).
6. "Microalgal cultivation for oxygen production using visible solar ray condensed by Fresnel lenses and transmitted through optical fibers," *Proceedings of The Second ISAS Space Utilization Symposium*, pp. 109–112 (June 3, 1985).
7. "Concept of 'Himawari' Marine Ranch," *Proceedings of Civil Engineering in the Ocean*, vol. **2**, pp. 7–11 (1986) (in Japanese).
8. "Photoautotrophic bioreactor using visible solar rays condensed by Fresnel lenses and transmitted through optical fibers," *Biotechnology and Bioengineering*, no. 15, pp. 331–345 (1986).
9. "Marine ranch concept using a visible solar ray condenser 'Himawari'," *The 1st. Japan Institute for Macro-Engineering Conference*, pp. 9–15 (February 13, 1986) (in Japanese).
10. "Sunlight supply and gas exchange systems in microalgal bioreactor," *Adv. Space Res.* vol. **7**, pp. 447–452 (1987).
11. "Solar energy utilizing technology for future cities," *Journal of The Fuel Society of Japan*, vol. **66**, no. 11, pp. 948–959 (1987) (in Japanese).

12. "A Marine ranch concept using the 'Himawari' automatic sunlight collection and distribution system, and actual marine experiments using this system," *8th Ocean Engineering Symposium of The Society of Naval Architects of Japan*, pp. 153–159 (January 20, 1988) (in Japanese).
13. "A marine ranch concept using a sunflower 'Himawari'," *Pacific Cooperation and Development*, pp. 109–118 (1988) (in Japanese).
14. "Gas exchange by chlorella with hydrophobic membrane," *Journal of The Japan Society for Aeronautical and Space Sciences*, vol. **36**, pp. 466–472 (October 1988) (in Japanese).
15. "Marine Development and Biotechnology," *Macro Review*, vol. **1**, no. 1, pp. 45–52 (1988) (in Japanese).
16. "Design for a bioreactor with sunlight supply and operations systems for use in the space environment," *Adv. Space Res.*, vol. **9**, no. 8, pp. 161–168 (1989).
17. "Application of a sunlight collection and distribution system in Marine Biotechnology," *The 1st International Marine Biotechnology Conference*, pp. 51 (September 4, 1989).
18. "Marinealgal cultivation system using solar bioreactor," *Proceedings of The Society of Formentation Technology Japan Symposium*, pp. 18 (1989).
19. "An underground office building and disaster shelter project," *Macro Review*, vol. **2**, no. 1; pp. 9–11 (1989) (in Japanese).
20. "Application of sunlight supply system in biotechnology," *Bioindustry*, vol. **6**, no. 5, pp. 329–336 (1989) (in Japanese).

THE SYMPOSIUM ON DYNAMIC ECONOMICS AND OTHER ASPECTS OF KEI MORI'S ECONOMETRIC RESEARCH

Kei Mori: His Life and Career in Economics

Chairman's Address by Tatsuhiko Kawashima (Gakushuin University, Tokyo, Japan)

It is my privilege to have been asked to serve today as a chairman at this "Symposium on Dynamic Economics and Other Aspects of Kei Mori's Econometric Research," in celebration of his new publication, *A Macroeconomic Simulation Analysis of the Post-War Japanese Economy, 1953–1961* (Yuhikaku, Tokyo, 1993). In performing my role, it is a great pleasure for me to open this meeting to honor the significant academic contributions by the late Professor Kei Mori in the field of economics, as well as to commemorate his marvelous warm-hearted personality.

With deep appreciation for this opportunity extended to me this morning, I would like to talk briefly about Kei, especially focusing upon the three aspects: (1) a chronological sketch of Kei's life, (2) Kei's scholarly relationships with Professor Lawrence R. Klein at the University of Pennsylvania, and (3) my personal association with Kei.

Aspect 1: Kei's life

Professor Kei Mori was born in Kyoto in 1932, as the first son of the late Mr. Taikichiro Mori, who taught at Yokohama City University until 1960, and has been counted among the first-rank scholars of Economics. He also became one of the most successful businessmen. On top of that he remains, in our memory, as a man of the soundest philosophy on the urban-redevelopment horizon, outstanding in that field.

Kei moved to the Kanto region when he was a junior high-school student. He received both undergraduate and graduate education at Keio University. In

1958, Kei was appointed as a faculty member of the School of Engineering of Keio University, an institution with which he had been continuously associated until the time he departed this life.

In the meantime, Kei married the well-educated and cultured lady Ms. Yoko Arisawa, in 1963. At that time, he had already established his reputation as one of the pioneers in Japanese econometrics. After his marriage, Kei obtained a doctorate in the field of economics from Keio University, in 1968. In the same year, he went to the US with Yoko and their one-and-a-half-year-old daughter, Mariko, as a visiting scholar at the Wharton School of the University of Pennsylvania to work with Professor Lawrence Klein. During their happy two-year stay in the suburbs of Philadelphia, in Pennsylvania, Kei carried out substantial and fruitful scientific research, while Yoko was studying the Northern Renaissance art as a graduate student of Bryn Mawr College. Their daughter was enjoying the precious experience of creative international interaction with children who came from various countries, including two daughters of Professor and Mrs. Mitsuo Saito, who were also at Pennsylvania then.

In 1970 Kei came back to Japan. His second daughter Asuka was born in 1973. Around that period he had completed a great deal of successful research in the field of dynamic properties of econometric models, management of data-processing, and utilization of the sun's rays related to his inventive engineering project of "Sunflowers" (*Himawari*). One of the main installations of *Himawari* is now placed at the Fujisawa Campus of Keio University. Further particulars about Kei's scientific records are listed on pages 413–416 of a book entitled *New Dimensions of Econometrics — Models, Simulation, and Network* (Yuhikaku, Tokyo, 1993) which has been published today as a collection of Kei's academic essays.

In February 1990, we suddenly lost Kei and his delightful personality. In the month of May of the same year, he was honored with the degree of D.Sc. (Doctor of Science) from the Carnegie Mellon University, which certainly provides clear additional evidence of his internationally acclaimed academic ability.

Aspect 2: Kei's scholarly relationships with Professor Lawrence R. Klein

Kei was working with Professor Klein at the University of Pennsylvania, from 1968 through 1970, on the subjects of (1) international and domestic economic impacts of the reduction of defense expenditures, (2) determination of eigen values of dynamic econometric systems, from the joint viewpoints of theoretical implications and mathematical tractability, and (3) a systems-analysis type of design for managing the data necessary for the conduct of Project LINK through a satellite telecommunication network.

In conjunction with Kei's research activities at Penn that were carried out together with Lawrie Klein I still have vivid impressions before my eyes of the image of the office room of the Econometric Research Unit, situated in the basement of the Dietrich Hall building of Penn, where he enjoyed pursuing his ingenious thoughts on adapting important sub-models of the gigantic Wharton Econometric Forecasting Model in order to make it more workable, to extract the characteristic roots of linear and non-linear dynamic equation systems, and to analyze the impacts of reduction of military expenditures for different scenarios on international disarmament programs, after the Vietnam War.

I feel sure that through these research activities, high-level intellectual interaction between Lawrie and Kei took place in the sphere of econometrics. Lawrie will perhaps talk later on, more about Kei at Penn, in his presentation at this symposium.

Aspect 3: My personal association with Kei

It is also my recollection that Kei often returned to the University after dinner to stay at the computer center until its closing hour at midnight. During the period when Kei was at Penn, among familiar figures at the computer center who regularly stayed until midnight were Professors Shinjo and Saito as well as myself. We frequently took a break together in a lounge room for computer users over cups of coffee, tea, or soft drinks. This common experience seems to have brought the four of us into closer association with each other.

It now comes to my mind that Kei kindly delivered to our apartment, for our daughter, a sack of charming sea shells on his way home from the Delaware beach, where he had personally collected them. This overlaps memories of Kei and Yoko inviting our family to their apartment to share joys of our life at Penn.

Be that as it may, Kei's life was short in terms of what we needed from him. But his life was beautifully intensive, blessed with his industrious research activities, and a huge bundle of poetic visions, always looking positively at the bright side of the future.

A quotation from a 17th century book entitled *Poetical Rhapsody* reads "Absence makes the heart grow fonder." I would like to conclude my address with respectful and warm sentiments toward Kei by saying: "Kei's absence makes our hearts fonder and fonder of him, a man of profound and humane character."

Achievement of the second career of Kei Mori — *Himawari*

DYNAMIC PROPERTIES OF AN ASSET MARKET MODEL

KAZUO OGAWA
Faculty of Economics, Kobe University

MITSUO SAITO
Faculty of Economics, Tezukayama University
7-1-1 Tezukayama NARA 631, Japan

and

ICHIRO TOKUTSU*
School of Business Administration, Kobe University

1. Introduction

Since the pioneering works by F. and I. Adelman (1959) and by Goldberger (1959), many contributions to the study of the dynamic properties of macro-econometric models have been published. The methods applied have been of a wide variety: Simulations, the extraction of characteristic roots, spectral analysis, etc. (e.g. [Evans–Klein–Saito, 1972]). The econometric models dealt with have been extended: linear, nonlinear, condensed version, full-fledged large-scale version, etc. [Mori, 1971], [Howrey, 1972]. The progress in computer facilities have made it possible to perform the analysis including an enormous amount of sophisticated calculations.

This study intends to analyze the dynamic properties of an asset market model. It may add a fresh experiment to the past studies of this field in the following way. First, the model treats the general equilibrium of asset

*The authors are grateful to Hidekazu Eguchi and Lawrence R. Klein for their illuminating discussions on both theoretical and empirical issues. They also wish to thank Toshiaki Ito for most helpful comments and suggestions on computational algorithms for solving characteristic equations. Responsibility for errors remains with the authors.

markets. Thus, the variables in the model are mostly stock variables, while they are dominated by flow variables in ordinary nation-wide econometric models. Second, stock adjustment in the portfolio equations is of the generalized version. Stock adjustment of each variable is made for the demands for all the assets in the system, satisfying the adding-up restraint. Third, we also mention the computational problems often encountered in obtaining characteristic roots, from a practical viewpoint.

Section 2 is devoted to a brief explanation of the model. Section 3 treats the examinations of the dynamic properties of the portfolio equations of each individual agent. In Sec. 4 the dynamic properties of the asset markets in the whole economy are analyzed. The results indicate the following findings: The asset market model is stable in the sense that the dynamic path, the exogenous variables being kept constant, converges to the long-run equilibrium values. The length of period of the convergence is only about 12 years, in spite of the relatively slow adjustment of the portfolio equation of nonfinancial corporate firms.

2. The Model

The model is, in principle, one of general equilibrium [Brainard–Tobin, 1968], [Tobin, 1969]. Let us first explain the standard form of the model in quite a general way.[a] The model consists of (1) the subjective equilibrium equations, or the portfolio equations of economic agents, and (2) the market equilibrium equations, or market clearing equations.

We assume that economic agents are categorized into seven groups: (1) Households, (2) Nonfinancial corporate firms(or simply Firms), (3) Private financial institutions (or simply Banks), (4) Government, (5) Public financial institutions, (6) the Bank of Japan, and (7) the Rest of the world. Sectors (4) through (7) are assumed to be exogenous.

Portfolio Equations of Individual Economic Agents of the Private Sector

The general formula of portfolio behavior is shown by the following system of equations:

$$\boldsymbol{A} = \boldsymbol{\alpha} W + \boldsymbol{\beta} Y + \boldsymbol{\Gamma} \boldsymbol{R}, \tag{1}$$

[a]For more detailed explanation of the model, see [Ogawa–Saito–Tokutsu, 1990].

$$W = \sum_{i=1}^{n} Ai\,, \tag{2}$$

where

$$\boldsymbol{A} = \begin{bmatrix} A1 \\ A2 \\ \vdots \\ An \end{bmatrix}, \quad \boldsymbol{R} = \begin{bmatrix} R1 \\ R2 \\ \vdots \\ Rn \end{bmatrix}, \quad \boldsymbol{\alpha} = \begin{bmatrix} \alpha_1 \\ \alpha_2 \\ \vdots \\ \alpha_n \end{bmatrix}, \quad \boldsymbol{\beta} = \begin{bmatrix} \beta_1 \\ \beta_2 \\ \vdots \\ \beta_n \end{bmatrix},$$

$$\boldsymbol{\Gamma} = \begin{bmatrix} \gamma_{11} & \gamma_{12} & \cdots & \gamma_{1n} \\ \gamma_{21} & \gamma_{22} & \cdots & \gamma_{2n} \\ \vdots & \vdots & \ddots & \vdots \\ \gamma_{n1} & \gamma_{n2} & \cdots & \gamma_{nn} \end{bmatrix}, \quad \text{and}$$

Ai = the end-of-period holdings of the ith asset (or liability),

Ri = the real rate of return of the ith asset (or liability),

W = the total of assets (and liabilities),

Y = the activity variable (income for households, sales for firms, deposits for banks),

$\boldsymbol{\alpha}$, $\boldsymbol{\beta}$, and $\boldsymbol{\Gamma}$ = parameters.

Adding-up restraints are shown as follows:

$$\boldsymbol{\alpha}'\boldsymbol{e} = 1\,, \quad \boldsymbol{\beta}'\boldsymbol{e} = 0\,, \quad \boldsymbol{\Gamma}'\boldsymbol{e} = \boldsymbol{0}\,, \tag{3}$$

where

$$\boldsymbol{e} = \begin{bmatrix} 1 \\ 1 \\ \vdots \\ 1 \end{bmatrix}$$

Equations (1) and (2) are static portfolio equations. Their dynamic version may be represented by the following system of equations:

$$\boldsymbol{A}_t = \boldsymbol{D}\boldsymbol{A}_{t-1} + \boldsymbol{a}W_t + \boldsymbol{b}Y_t + \boldsymbol{C}\boldsymbol{R}_t\,, \tag{4}$$

$$W_t = \sum_{i=1}^{n} Ai_t\,, \tag{5}$$

$$\boldsymbol{D} = \begin{bmatrix} d_{11} & d_{12} & \cdots & d_{1n} \\ d_{21} & d_{22} & \cdots & d_{2n} \\ \vdots & \vdots & \ddots & \vdots \\ d_{n1} & d_{n2} & \cdots & d_{nn} \end{bmatrix}$$

$$\boldsymbol{a}'\boldsymbol{e} = 1\,, \quad \boldsymbol{b}'\boldsymbol{e} = 0\,, \quad \boldsymbol{C}'\boldsymbol{e} = \boldsymbol{0}\,, \quad \boldsymbol{D}'\boldsymbol{e} = \boldsymbol{0}\,, \tag{6}$$

where $\boldsymbol{A}_t$, $\boldsymbol{R}_t$, $\boldsymbol{a}$, $\boldsymbol{b}$, and $\boldsymbol{C}$ have the same dimensions as $\boldsymbol{A}$, $\boldsymbol{R}$, $\boldsymbol{\alpha}$, $\boldsymbol{\beta}$, and $\boldsymbol{\Gamma}$, respectively.

Equation (4) is derived by assuming the following stock adjustment process in portfolio behavior:

$$\boldsymbol{A}_t - \boldsymbol{A}_{t-1} = \boldsymbol{D}^*(\boldsymbol{A}_t^* - \boldsymbol{A}_{t-1})\,, \tag{7}$$

$$\boldsymbol{A}_t^* = \boldsymbol{\alpha}W_t = \boldsymbol{\beta}Y_t + \boldsymbol{\Gamma}\boldsymbol{R}_t\,, \tag{8}$$

$$\boldsymbol{D}^* = \begin{bmatrix} d_{11}^* & d_{12}^* & \cdots & d_{1n}^* \\ d_{21}^* & d_{22}^* & \cdots & d_{2n}^* \\ \vdots & \vdots & \ddots & \vdots \\ d_{n1}^* & d_{n2}^* & \cdots & d_{nn}^* \end{bmatrix},$$

where

$$\boldsymbol{D} = \boldsymbol{I} - \boldsymbol{D}^*\,, \quad \boldsymbol{a} = \boldsymbol{D}^*\boldsymbol{\alpha}\,, \quad \boldsymbol{b} = \boldsymbol{D}^*\boldsymbol{\beta}\,, \quad \text{and} \quad \boldsymbol{C} = \boldsymbol{D}^*\boldsymbol{\Gamma}\,. \tag{9}$$

The system of Eqs. (4) are estimated by pooling the panel and the time series data of agents. That is to say, we estimate $\boldsymbol{\alpha}$, $\boldsymbol{\beta}$, and $\boldsymbol{D}$ based on panel data for individual households, banks, and firms, and then using these parameters we estimate $\boldsymbol{C}$ from the time series of the sectoral balance-sheet accounts.[b] Estimated adjustment coefficients of Eq. (4) are shown in Tables 1 (Households), 2 (Banks), and 3 (Firms).[c]

Table 1. Estimated Adjustment Coefficients of Households

	(1) *hA*11	(2) *hA*12	(3) *hA*2	(4) *hA*82	(5) *hA*4	(6) *hA*3	(7) *hA*81	(8) *hA*61	(9) *hA*62
(1) *hA*11 : currency	**0.418**	0.010	0.003	-0.010	-0.020	-0.025	-0.004	-0.023	-0.011
(2) *hA*12 : demand deposits	-0.014	**0.400**	0.005	-0.020	-0.038	-0.047	-0.007	-0.044	-0.021
(3) *hA*2 : time deposits	-0.053	-0.026	**0.547**	-0.102	-0.183	-0.211	-0.078	-0.121	-0.099
(4) *hA*82 : life insurance	-0.009	-0.005	-0.020	**0.512**	-0.036	-0.046	-0.082	-0.051	-0.036
(5) *hA*4 : shares	-0.031	-0.079	-0.100	-0.068	**0.694**	-0.080	-0.012	-0.099	-0.076
(6) *hA*3 : bonds	0.007	0.003	-0.038	-0.051	-0.056	**0.783**	-0.033	-0.026	-0.018
(7) *hA*81 : other financial assets	-0.033	-0.017	-0.021	-0.019	-0.014	-0.034	**0.664**	-0.023	-0.018
(8) *hA*61 : bank loans	-0.185	-0.176	-0.274	-0.212	-0.251	-0.235	-0.237	**0.502**	-0.293
(9) *hA*62 : other loans	-0.099	-0.111	-0.103	-0.031	-0.095	-0.107	-0.212	-0.115	**0.572**

Table 2. Estimated Adjustment Coefficients of Banks

	(1) *bA*9	(2) *bA*11	(3) *bA*12	(4) *bA*3	(5) *bA*4	(6) *bA*51	(7) *bA*6	(8) *bA*7	(9) *bA*52	(10) *bA*8
(1) *bA*9 : real assets	**0.654**	-0.005	-0.006	-0.003	-0.031	-0.006	-0.004	0.012	-0.005	0.001
(2) *bA*11 : currency	0.504	**0.333**	-0.082	-0.082	-0.147	-0.006	-0.080	-0.056	0.012	0.075
(3) *bA*12 : deposits at the BOJ	0.016	0.187	**0.470**	-0.177	0.245	0.009	-0.180	-0.215	-0.455	0.109
(4) *bA*3 : bonds	-0.603	-0.006	-0.087	**0.647**	-0.303	0.029	-0.112	-0.157	-0.231	0.018
(5) *bA*4 : shares	-0.031	-0.020	-0.067	-0.001	**0.687**	0.007	-0.022	0.036	0.057	-0.078
(6) *bA*51 : call loans	-0.078	-0.169	-0.001	-0.056	0.061	**0.179**	-0.040	-0.001	-0.121	0.041
(7) *bA*6 : bank loans	-0.537	-0.235	-0.138	-0.309	-0.157	-0.181	**0.498**	-0.337	-0.134	-0.454
(8) *bA*7 : loans from the BOJ	-0.174	-0.040	0.033	-0.010	0.036	0.003	-0.003	**0.709**	0.023	0.028
(9) *bA*52 : call money	0.226	0.026	-0.015	0.016	-0.310	-0.046	0.024	0.046	**0.657**	0.035
(10) *bA*8 : other net liabilities	0.023	-0.071	-0.109	-0.024	-0.080	0.011	-0.082	-0.038	0.199	**0.226**

[b] The panel data estimation for $\boldsymbol{D}$, $\boldsymbol{a}$, and $\boldsymbol{b}$ is based on OLS with constant dummy variables in order to take into account the households', banks', or firms' own effects (Fixed Effect Model) and $\boldsymbol{C}$ is estimated from the time series data by SUR with adding-up restraints. In the panel data analysis, precisely speaking, the net worth W is not an exogenous variable, so OLS may lead to biased estimates. See [Summers, 1959].

[c] These tables show estimates only of the adjustment coefficients. For the coefficients of net worth, activity variable, and the rates of return, see [Ogawa–Saito–Tokutsu, 1990]. The number of assets and liabilities is slightly different among the agents, owing to economic reasons. The details are shown in [Saito–Oshika, 1977], [Saito–Ogawa–Tokutsu, 1988], and [Ogawa–Saito–Tokutsu, 1988] for households, banks, and nonfinancial firms, respectively.

Table 3. Estimated Adjustment Coefficients of Firms

	(1) *fA*91	(2) *fA*92	(3) *fA*93	(4) *fA*1	(5) *fA*2	(6) *fA*31	(7) *fA*4	(8) *fA*61	(9) *fA*32	(10) *fA*62	(11) *fA*63	(12) *fA*8
(1) *fA*91 : inventories	**0.528**	-0.084	0.224	0.056	0.025	-0.027	-0.035	-0.034	-0.036	-0.034	-0.024	-0.020
(2) *fA*92 : gross capital stock	-0.129	**0.735**	-0.008	-0.133	-0.088	-0.076	-0.118	-0.188	-0.121	-0.153	-0.190	-0.028
(3) *fA*93 : land, etc	-0.016	-0.006	**0.692**	-0.003	-0.008	-0.013	-0.019	-0.028	-0.025	-0.021	-0.035	-0.018
(4) *fA*1 : currency and demand deposits	-0.072	-0.088	-0.122	**0.317**	-0.120	-0.060	-0.074	-0.074	-0.056	-0.079	-0.110	-0.161
(5) *fA*2 : time deposits	-0.128	-0.118	-0.130	-0.070	**0.439**	-0.101	-0.125	-0.114	-0.073	-0.156	-0.140	-0.089
(6) *fA*31 : bonds(assets)	-0.049	-0.063	-0.041	-0.033	-0.028	**0.541**	-0.048	-0.052	-0.035	-0.048	-0.062	-0.020
(7) *fA*4 : shares	-0.209	-0.193	-0.248	-0.167	-0.191	-0.177	**0.473**	-0.235	-0.135	-0.220	-0.235	-0.126
(8) *fA*61 : trade credit	-0.193	-0.154	-0.144	-0.025	-0.105	-0.142	-0.142	**0.409**	-0.071	-0.149	-0.008	-0.126
(9) *fA*32 : bonds(liability)	-0.026	-0.041	-0.059	-0.011	-0.022	0.002	-0.032	-0.026	**0.740**	-0.034	-0.023	-0.031
(10) *fA*62 : bank loans	0.089	-0.018	0.011	0.022	0.079	-0.019	0.014	0.226	0.028	**0.856**	0.294	-0.008
(11) *fA*63 : trade debt	0.229	0.080	-0.023	0.089	0.015	0.027	0.087	0.207	0.009	0.107	**0.665**	0.022
(12) *fA*8 : other net liabilities	-0.023	-0.050	-0.152	-0.041	0.004	0.047	0.020	-0.092	-0.225	-0.069	-0.133	**0.602**

3. The Dynamic Property of the Portfolio Equations

Simulation

There are several methods for examining the dynamic properties of the system of simultaneous difference equations (4) and (5). In this study let us adopt two methods: (1) to simulate the model, and (2) to solve the characteristic equation. It is known that, if the system of Eqs. (4) and (5) is stable, $\boldsymbol{A}_t$ approaches $\boldsymbol{A}_t^*$ in Eq. (8), provided that W_t, Y_t, and $\boldsymbol{R}_t$ are fixed at $\overline{W}_t$, $\overline{Y}_t$, and $\overline{\boldsymbol{R}}_t$, respectively. The stability of Eqs. (4) and (5) holds if the calculated value of $\boldsymbol{D}^t$ approaches $\boldsymbol{0}$. Now, the results of the calculations reveal the fact that $\boldsymbol{D}^t$ approaches the zero matrix for all the three cases of households, firms, and banks, as t increases indefinitely. Table 4 gives the number of years n, in which all the elements of $\boldsymbol{D}^t$ turn out to be less than 0.1. This number is 31, 9, and 10 for firms, banks, and households, respectively, indicating that the length of time in reaching the equilibrium values is the longest for firms. The slow convergence for firms may be ascribed to the following facts of the Japanese economy:

(1) It is well known that the period of stock adjustment is longer in fixed capital than in financial assets.[d] In fact the calculation for the matrix deleting capital stock shows that the number of years for convergence decreases from 31 to 19. In our portfolio model, the assets of households, with a convergence period of 10 years, do not include the stock of real assets(houses), owing to the lack of data availability in the panel sample.

(2) Japanese firms mutually own a large amount of shares and bonds of other firms within a particular group of firms. This practice is effective for stabilizing stock prices and avoiding take over bids. Therefore, bonds and shares held by corporate firms for this purpose are rarely offered for sale, introducing rigidity in portfolio selection of firms.

(3) Japanese firms owe much of their funds for plant and equipment to banks, whose credit amounts are more or less fixed for a long-term. This part of the portfolio of firms tends to be rigid.

[d] In his insightful paper, Sato [Sato, 1963] pointed out the fact that in Solow's growth model it will take 100 years to approach the equilibrium state reasonably well.

Table 4. The Number of Periods in Which All the Elements of $\boldsymbol{A}^t$ Become Less than 0.1

Households	Banks	Firms
10	9	31

Table 5. The Characteristic Roots of the Portfolio Equations of Households, Banks, and Firms

Households

	Real part	Imaginary part	Absolute value
1	0.815495		0.815495
2	0.781688		0.781688
3	0.758824		0.758824
4	0.668067	0.012959	0.668193
5	0.668067	-0.012959	0.668193
6	0.552651		0.552651
7	0.436711		0.436711
8	0.409897		0.409897

Banks

	Real part	Imaginary part	Absolute value
1	0.784115		0.784115
2	0.738768		0.738768
3	0.661108	0.222396	0.697512
4	0.661108	-0.222396	0.697512
5	0.682425	0.044712	0.683888
6	0.682425	-0.044712	0.683888
7	0.350978	0.109035	0.367524
8	0.350978	-0.109035	0.367524
9	0.148098		0.148098

Firms

	Real part	Imaginary part	Absolute value
1	0.942303		0.942303
2	0.795023		0.795023
3	0.776131		0.776131
4	0.692655		0.692655
5	0.656013	0.012786	0.656138
6	0.656013	-0.012786	0.656138
7	0.559929	0.020966	0.560321
8	0.559929	-0.020966	0.560321
9	0.543187		0.543187
10	0.465100		0.465100
11	0.353717		0.353717

The Characteristic Roots of Difference Equations

The dynamic properties of the system of difference equations (4) and (5) are also revealed by the calculation of the characteristic roots of the system. The results for households, banks, and firms are shown in Table 5.[e] The absolute values of the roots are all less than unity, implying stability of the dynamic system. It is found that the absolute values of the largest root in firms, 0.942, is close to unity, being consistent with the relatively slow convergence of $\boldsymbol{D}^t$ to zero. The imaginary (conjugate complex) roots are observed in all three sectors: one, three and two sets in households, banks, and firms, respectively. It is to be noted, however, that the absolute values of all the imaginary roots are not large, being mainly in the range (0.37, 0.70). In fact, the simulation of the system also shows only slight oscillation for all three sectors.

Notes to the Calculation Methods of the Characteristic Roots

It has frequently been pointed out that the extraction of characteristic roots is subject to a subtle computational problem. (e.g. [Howrey, 1972], pp. 636 and 654). It is also generally recognized among practitioners of computer calculation that if the characteristic roots are near unity or zero, the results are very susceptible to rounding errors. Unfortunately, it is often observed that most econometric models include roots close to unity. In addition, as is seen from Table 5, the adjustment coefficient matrix of the asset demand equations, $\boldsymbol{D}$, is not symmetric. Most of the algorithms for obtaining the characteristic roots, however, assume symmetry of the matrix.

The algorithm we adopted in this study is the *Double QR method*.[f] This algorithm is one of the most reliable ones which can treat the asymmetric structure of the matrix. Let us explain this method briefly. The basic idea of this method is to transform the original matrix to an upper diagonal matrix whose diagonal elements are equivalent to the characteristic roots to be obtained. That is to say, the original matrix, $\boldsymbol{D}^{(1)}\,(=\boldsymbol{D})$ can be uniquely decomposed into the product of $\boldsymbol{Q}^{(1)}$ and $\boldsymbol{R}^{(1)}$ as:

$$\boldsymbol{D}^{(1)} = \boldsymbol{Q}^{(1)}\boldsymbol{R}^{(1)}\,,$$

[e]The number of non-zero characteristic roots is the number of assets and liabilities minus unity, since the adding up restraints reduce the number of independent equations in the portfolio system by one.

[f]For detailed description of this numerical method, see Wilkinson (1965).

where $\boldsymbol{Q}^{(1)}$ is the Unitary Matrix and $\boldsymbol{R}^{(1)}$ is an upper diagonal matrix. Using these $\boldsymbol{Q}^{(1)}$ and $\boldsymbol{R}^{(1)}$, $\boldsymbol{D}^{(1)}$ is transformed to

$$\boldsymbol{D}^{(2)} = \boldsymbol{R}^{(1)}\boldsymbol{Q}^{(1)} .$$

If this transformation is iterated indefinitely, it is known that $\boldsymbol{D}^{(k)}$ approaches the upper diagonal matrix and the diagonal elements of $D^{(k)}$ approach the characteristic roots of $\boldsymbol{D}^{(1)}\,(=\boldsymbol{D})$ as $k \rightarrow \infty$. The use of the Unitary Matrix in the transformation makes it possible to treat the complex structure of the characteristic roots. In the actual computation, in order to simplify the iteration process, the original matrix $\boldsymbol{D}$ is transformed in advance to the Hessenberg Matrix before iteration.

As we stated before, the Double QR method is one of the most reliable algorithms presently available, but it still has some practical problems in the convergence of the iteration process and in the uniqueness of QR decomposition. However, the characteristic roots obtained are all consistent with the simulation results. This means that the adoption of this algorithm is quite appropriate for our model.

4. The Dynamic Properties of the Market Equations

The asset market model assumes that all the real rates of return are determined so as to clear the excess demand or supply simultaneously in all the markets of individual assets and liabilities.

The excess demand for each asset is defined as

$$\boldsymbol{A}_t^h + \boldsymbol{A}_t^b + \boldsymbol{A}_t^f + \boldsymbol{F}_t\,, \tag{10}$$

where

$$\boldsymbol{F}_t = \begin{bmatrix} F_{1t} \\ F_{2t} \\ \vdots \\ F_{nt} \end{bmatrix}$$

Superscripts attached to $\boldsymbol{A}_t$, i.e., h, b, and f, represent the agents that hold assets: households, banks and firms. $\boldsymbol{F}_t$ is a vector of the demand for each asset and liability from the exogenous sectors: Government, Public financial institutions, the Bank of Japan, and the Rest of the world.

The market clearing equations may be shown by:

$$\boldsymbol{A}_t^h + \boldsymbol{A}_t^b + \boldsymbol{A}_t^f + \boldsymbol{F}_t = \boldsymbol{0}\,. \tag{11}$$

The market equilibrium in the economy as a whole may be represented by the solution of a set of simultaneous equations, which consists of Eq. (11) and the following portfolio equations of each agent:

$$\boldsymbol{A}_t^h = \boldsymbol{D}^h \boldsymbol{A}_{t-1}^h + \boldsymbol{g}_t^h + \boldsymbol{C}^h \boldsymbol{R}_t\,, \tag{12}$$

$$\boldsymbol{A}_t^b = \boldsymbol{D}^b \boldsymbol{A}_{t-1}^b + \boldsymbol{g}_t^b + \boldsymbol{C}^b \boldsymbol{R}_t\,, \tag{13}$$

$$\boldsymbol{A}_t^f = \boldsymbol{D}^f \boldsymbol{A}_{t-1}^f + \boldsymbol{g}_t^f + \boldsymbol{C}^f \boldsymbol{R}_t\,, \tag{14}$$

where

$$\boldsymbol{g}_t^j = \boldsymbol{a}^j W_t^j + \boldsymbol{b}^j Y_t^j\,. \tag{15}$$

Here j is h, b, or f. That is to say, $\boldsymbol{g}_t^j$ stands for the exogenous part of the system. Again, superscripts identify the agents.

The system of simultaneous equations may be represented in matrix notation by:

$$\begin{bmatrix} 0 & \boldsymbol{I} & \boldsymbol{I} & \boldsymbol{I} \\ -\boldsymbol{C}^h & \boldsymbol{I} & \boldsymbol{0} & \boldsymbol{0} \\ -\boldsymbol{C}^b & \boldsymbol{0} & \boldsymbol{I} & \boldsymbol{0} \\ -\boldsymbol{C}^f & \boldsymbol{0} & \boldsymbol{0} & \boldsymbol{I} \end{bmatrix} \begin{bmatrix} \boldsymbol{R}_t \\ \boldsymbol{A}_t^h \\ \boldsymbol{A}_t^b \\ \boldsymbol{A}_t^f \end{bmatrix}$$

$$= \begin{bmatrix} \boldsymbol{0} & \boldsymbol{0} & \boldsymbol{0} & \boldsymbol{0} \\ \boldsymbol{0} & \boldsymbol{D}^h & \boldsymbol{0} & \boldsymbol{0} \\ \boldsymbol{0} & \boldsymbol{0} & \boldsymbol{D}^b & \boldsymbol{0} \\ \boldsymbol{0} & \boldsymbol{0} & \boldsymbol{0} & \boldsymbol{D}^f \end{bmatrix} \begin{bmatrix} \boldsymbol{R}_{t-1} \\ \boldsymbol{A}_{t-1}^h \\ \boldsymbol{A}_{t-1}^b \\ \boldsymbol{A}_{t-1}^f \end{bmatrix} + \begin{bmatrix} -\boldsymbol{F}_t \\ \boldsymbol{g}_t^h \\ \boldsymbol{g}_t^b \\ \boldsymbol{g}_t^f \end{bmatrix}. \tag{16}$$

The construction of the empirical general equilibrium model is described in Table 6. Column (1) shows that the excess demand for asset $\boldsymbol{A}_t$ is the sum of holdings by households ($\boldsymbol{A}_t^h$), banks ($\boldsymbol{A}_t^b$), and firms ($\boldsymbol{A}_t^f$). Column (2) presents the rate of return corresponding to each asset. Columns (3), (4), and (5) give the composition of the excess demand for each asset. For example, currency and demand deposits held by households, $A1_t^h$, consist of holdings of currency ($hA11_t$) and of demand deposits ($hA12_t$).

By wealth restraint, holdings of currency and demand deposits are derived from holdings of all the other assets. Therefore, the equilibrium equation for currency and demand deposits, $A1_t^h + A1_t^b + A1_t^f = 0$, is neglected in the determination of the rates of return. Also, $R1_t$ is not defined. It is further assumed that the interest rate on time deposits, $R2_t$, is exogenously given, and holdings of time deposits are supplied by banks to the extent that households and firms want such deposits. Thus, the equilibrium equation for time deposits, $A2_t^h + A2_t^b + A2_t^f = 0$, is also neglected in the determination of the rates of return.

In all, seven rates of return, Ri_t $(i = 3, \ldots, 9)$, are determined by seven equilibrium equations,

$$Ai_t^h + Ai_t^b + Ai_t^f = 0\,, \quad (i = 3, \ldots, 9)\,.$$

Table 6. The Scheme of the General Equilibrium Model

	(1) $A^h_t+A^b_t+A^f_t$ assets	(2) R_t rates of return	(3) A^h_t households	(4) A^b_t banks	(5) A^f_t firms
(1)	$A1$: currency and demand deposits	$R1$:	$hA11+hA12$	$bA11+bA12$	$fA1$
(2)	$A2$: time depostis	$R2$: interest rate on time deposits	$hA2$		$fA2$
(3)	$A3$: bonds	$R3$: bond yield	$hA3$	$bA3$	$fA31+fA32$
(4)	$A4$: shares	$R4$: rate of return on shares	$hA4$	$bA4$	$fA4$
(5)	$A5$: call loan and call money	$R5$: call rate		$bA51+bA52$	
(6)	$A6$: bank loans	$R6$: bank loan rate	$hA61+hA62$	$bA6$	$fA61+fA62+fA63$
(7)	$A7$: loans from the BOJ	$R7$: discount rate		$bA7$	
(8)	$A8$: other net liabilities	$R8$: rate of return on foreign assets	$hA81+hA82$	$bA8$	$fA8$
(9)	$A9$: real assets	$R9$: rate of return on real assets		$bA9$	$fA91+fA92+fA93$

For notations of $jA1, jA2$ ($j=h, b, f$), etc., in Columns (3), (4), and (5), see Tables 1 to 3.

The Stability of the Asset Market Model

The dynamic properties of the asset market model are examined both by the calculation of the characteristic roots and the simulation method. Specifically, we investigate the characteristic roots of the reduced form of the difference equation system (16). The results are shown in Table 7. The number of non-zero characteristic roots should be 18 because the number of independent equations is 18, as is seen from Table 6. Actually, 18 non-zero characteristic roots are obtained by the algorithm we adopt, but seven characteristic roots are extremely close to zero, although they can apparently be distinguished from zero. So we tabulate only eleven characteristic roots in Table 7. However, it turns out that the eleven characteristic roots obtained are all less than unity in absolute value. In fact, the iterative multiplication of the adjustment coefficient matrix of the reduced form reveals that all the elements of the matrix become less than 0.1 after 12 iterations. Both results imply the stability of our asset market model.

Table 7. The Characteristic Roots of the Market Clearing Equations

	Real part	Imaginary part	Absolute value
1	0.835539		0.835539
2	0.751902	0.026685	0.752375
3	0.751902	-0.026685	0.752375
4	0.710253	0.059759	0.712763
5	0.710253	-0.059759	0.712763
6	0.706171		0.706171
7	0.633784		0.633784
8	0.549520		0.549520
9	0.455577		0.455577
10	0.437587		0.437587
11	0.432640		0.432640

5. Concluding Remarks

The dynamic properties of the asset market model is examined by simulations and the calculations of the characteristic roots of the system. The model has the feature that the portfolio equations are of the Brainard–Tobin type with generalized stock adjustment, and most of the variables are stock variables instead of flow variables. The results reveal the fact that both systems of portfolio equations and of market clearing equations are stable; although the adjustment in the quantity of capital stock leads to a longer period of convergence to long-run equilibrium.

References

1. F. Adelman, and I. Adelman, "The dynamic properties of the Klein–Goldberger model," *Econometrica* **27**, pp. 596–625 (1959).
2. W. C. Brainard and J. Tobin "Pitfalls in financial model building," *American Economic Review, Papers and Proceedings* **85**, pp. 99–122 (1968).
3. M. K. Evans, L. R. Klein, and M. Saito, "Short-run prediction and long-run simulation of the Wharton model," in ed. B. Hickman, *Econometric Models of Cyclical Behavior* (Columbia University Press, New York, 1972), pp. 139–86.
4. A. S. Goldberger, *Impact Multipliers and Dynamic Properties of the Klein–Goldberger Model* (North-Holland, Amsterdam, 1959).
5. E. P. Howrey, "Dynamic properties of a condensed version of the Wharton model," in ed. B. Hickman, *Econometric Models of Cyclical Behavior* (Columbia University Press, New York, 1972), pp. 601–671.
6. K. Mori, "Generalized eigenvalue problem of an econometric model," *Econometrica* **39**, pp. 193–95 (1971).
7. K. Ogawa, M. Saito, and I. Tokutsu, "The flow-of-funds equations of Japanese nonfinancial firms," *Journal of the Japanese and International Economies* **8**, pp. 72–105 (1988).
8. K. Ogawa, M. Saito, and I. Tokutsu, "A general equilibrium approach to the Japanese asset markets," paper presented at the 6th World Congress of the Econometric Society, Barcelona, Spain, August 1990. Working Paper #9013, School of Business Administration, Kobe University (1990).
9. M. Saito, K. Ogawa, and I. Tokutsu, "The flow-of-funds equations of Japanese banks," paper presented at the Far Eastern Meeting of the Econometric Society, Tokyo, Japan, October 1987. Working Paper #8708, Faculty of Economics, Kobe University (1988). Forthcoming in ed. M. J. Dutta, *Economics, Econometrics and the LINK: Festschrift in Honor of Lawrence R. Klein.*
10. M. Saito, and T. Oshika, "Kakei no shisan juyo hoteishiki no keisoku (Estimation of the households' asset demand equations)," *Keizai Bunseki* **68**, pp. 1–34 (1977) (in Japanese).
11. R. Sato, "Fiscal policy in a neo-classical growth model: An analysis of time required for equilibrium adjustment," *Review of Economic Studies* **30**, pp. 16–23 (1963).
12. R. Summers, "A note on least squares bias in household expenditure analysis," *Econometrica* **27**, pp. 121–26 (1959).
13. J. Tobin, "A general equilibrium approach to monetary theory," *Journal of Money, Credit, and Banking* **1**, pp. 15–29 (1969).
14. J. H. Wilkinson, *The Algebraic Eigenvalue Problem* (Oxford University Press, London, 1965).

COMMENTS ON KAZUO OGAWA, MITSUO SAITO, AND ICHIRO TOKUTSU'S "DYNAMIC PROPERTIES OF AN ASSET MARKET MODEL"

HIDEKAZU EGUCHI
Tokyo International University

The purpose of this paper is to examine the dynamic properties of an econometric model of the Brainard–Tobin type.

First of all, the feature of this econometric model must be discussed briefly. Although such a discussion is not a task allotted to the commentator, the examination of the dynamic properties of the model is related to the special character of the model.

I think that the authors' econometric model is a splendid one. As far as he knows, it is the only example of a successfully estimated Brainard–Tobin model. The full-fledged Brainard–Tobin model is very hard to estimate, because each portfolio equation has many explanatory variables, and multicollinearity makes its estimation an extremely difficult job. The authors succeeded in the estimation by having recourse to pooling panel data and time series data. In particular, they executed a formidable task by utilizing a large volume of panel data for each of the three economic agents: households, nonfinancial firms, and banks.[a] In addition, the movement of the rates of return of all the assets and liabilities is beautifully traced in the within-sample simulation.[b]

[a] For detailed description of the procedures and the results of their estimation for each sector, see [Saito–Oshika, 1977], [Ogawa–Saito–Tokutsu, 1988], and [Saito–Ogawa–Tokutsu, 1988] referred to in their paper in this volume.

[b] They present graphically the results of the dynamic simulation in their 1990 paper.

My comments consist of three points. First, the authors' finding that the model is stable is novel, since it is different from stylized macro-econometric models. In this model each economic agent has a set of portfolio equations as follows:

$$\boldsymbol{A}_t = \boldsymbol{D}\boldsymbol{A}_{t-1} + \boldsymbol{a}W_t + \boldsymbol{b}Y_t + \boldsymbol{C}\boldsymbol{R}_t \, , \tag{4}$$

where A_t is a vector of holdings of each asset for each agent; W_t and Y_t are, respectively, net worth and an activity variable for each agent; R_t is a vector of rates of return. D and C are coefficient matrices; a and b are coefficient vectors.

The authors have already found for each agent that the system of portfolio equations is stable. The asset market model, however, is a model in which the excess demands of all the assets and liabilities are simultaneously cleared by the adjustments of their rates of return. This paper treats the behavior of the rates of return in such an asset market model. The authors find that the whole market is stable. This is clearly a new finding.

Second, the asset market model of the whole economy consists of a set of simultaneous difference equations. The authors examine its dynamic properties by two different approaches; by simulation and by extraction of the characteristic roots. The paper states that the simulation approach has practically no problems; the numerical calculation by double precision guarantees the necessary precision for possible size of rounding errors. Concerning the extraction of the characteristic roots, however, it is known that the calculation is not as easy a task as it looks, especially for econometric models. In fact, some twenty years ago, the late Kei Mori devoted much energy to this problem and did pioneering work on it. The essence of the authors' point in this paper is that the difficulty of the calculation of the characteristic roots of econometric models arises from two sources: the existence of roots close to unity or zero and the asymmetry of the coefficient matrix.[c] It is known that the existence of the characteristic roots near unity or zero presents risks in the calculation, and econometric models often have such a root. It is also known that in the case of a symmetric matrix a number of computer algorithms for solving the characteristic equation have been prepared. But this is not the case for an asymmetric matrix, which is also quite usual for econometric models, including the authors' models. The authors specify an algorithm, i.e., the *Double*

[c]This difficulty becomes more serious for a large scale econometric model in which the order of the characteristic equation is very high, as is the case with their model.

OR method, as the best available for treating the two problems above. This is a very useful, practical finding.

Third, the model is essentially an equilibrium model. In each period (year) the market reaches a temporary equilibrium. The movement of the rates of return of all the assets and liabilities is regarded as a successive continuation of such temporary equilibria. This paper is concerned with the dynamic properties of such a movement.

As a final comment of their paper, I would like to mention a recent phenomenon observed in Japanese asset markets, especially in the stock and land markets in conjunction with the authors' asset market model, since their model typically includes the above two asset markets. At the beginning of 1990, stock prices and land prices fell precipitously after a long spell of price rise in the preceding period, starting in 1987. This is called the "Bubble" or "Collapse of the Bubble." Can the authors' model fully explain the "Bubble" and its collapse? It must be a process of disequilibrium.

Temporarily, equilibrium for each period in this model is established on the grounds that in the portfolio equations people's expectations are static and that the whole system is one of gross substitutes. I think, with the authors, that static expectation, which assume the continuation of the present level in the future, is a simple and realistic assumption. People are inclined to expect that if the Giants win today, they will win tomorrow, too. In the midst of the Bubble period, however, people's expectations clearly were not static; they expected that a rise in an asset price today would lead to a further rise tomorrow, but would not keep today's level. In economic terms, the expectation in the "Bubble" period was that the elasticity of expectation of asset prices is larger than unity. In such a situation the higher the asset price, the larger is the demand for the asset; the asset market becomes unstable.[d]

The discrepancy of the implied expectation of the model from reality in the Bubble period would constitute a limitation to the applicability of the authors' model.

[d]The authors may argue that ordinarily such a volatile phenomenon does not continue for long. A yearly average static expectation might bring about temporary equilibrium, and the annual model might describe a year-to-year movement of the rates of return. However, within one period (year) or even over a couple of periods in a prolonged boom, like a "Bubble," the analysis based on static expectation is definitely inappropriate.

DYNAMIC PROPERTIES OF TCER AND RELATED MODELS

HIROYUKI KOSAKA
Administrative Engineering
Faculty of Science & Technology, Keio University
3-14-1 Hiyoshi, Kohoku-ku, Yokohama 223
Japan

1. Introduction

In this article I try to trace the core part of the late Prof. Mori's business cycle research, keeping in mind the interests of academic economics. This covers the 1960s, when both the US and Japanese economies were enjoying high economic growth. In connection with Prof. Mori's work, I will take the TCER model (Tokyo Center Economic Research Model), and the Wharton model. The LINK Project began in 1969. This decade was fruitful for econometric model building. I think current model building techniques owe much to the research undertaken in this decade.

2. Observed Cycles and Business Cycle Models

I will briefly review empirically observed cycles and their corresponding analytical business cycle models. The following cycles have been found empirically during the last century. (see Table 1) Typical observed cycles are presented in Table 1 [K. Inada and H. Uzawa, 1972], [M. Shinohara, 1980]. They are Kondratieff, Kuznets, Juglar, and Kitchin cycles.

The Kondratieff cycle is about 50 years in duration, and J. Schumpeter tried to describe the long wave in terms of innovation together with Juglar and Kitchin cycles [J. A. Schumpeter, 1939]. His theory is descriptive, and not in mathematical form. Once R. Frisch tried to formulate Schumpeter's theory in mathematical form, but Shumpeter was critical [R. Frisch, 1933]. Quite recently R. M. Goodwin formulated innovation theory using chaotic dynamics [R. M. Goodwin, 1990]. Also real business cycles theorists in the 1980s have been focussing on innovation. Generally, most economists do not take deep interest in the Kondratieff cycle, and political scientists like to refer to the long wave in connection with war [A. Tanaka, 1989]. It must be noted that war affects a domestic economy, and conversely some kinds of economic troubles will cause a war. The Kondratieff cycle seems to raise issues of importance in current times.

Table 1. Business Cycles and Business Cycle Models

Observed Cycles	Period	Source	Typical Theoretical Models
Kondratieff Cycle	50 yrs.	Innovation War	J. Schumpeter(1939) R. M. Goodwin(1990)
Kuznets Cycle	20 yrs.	Construction	
Juglar Cycle	7–10yrs.	Fixed Investment	P. Samuelson(1939) J. R. Hicks(1950) R. M. Goodwin(1951)
Kitchin Cycle	40 mos.	Inventory Investment	L. A. Metzler(1941) A. Medio(1992)
Political Cycle	not regular	Domestic International	W. D. Nordhaus(1975)

The Kuznets cycle is about 20 years in duration, and it is said to be related to construction, which is affected by demographic factors, i.e., increase of population and immigration. For the Kuznets cycle, time series analysts pose questions from the point of view of spectral analysis [G. S. Fishman, 1969]. I. Adelman gave us the article "Long Swing: Fact or Artifact?"

The Juglar cycle is the oldest one, which was first found in the latter part of the last century by a French economist. The period of the cycle is 7–10 years, which was caused by private fixed investment. Many economists feel challenged to formulate the underlying theory. A typical one is P. Samuelson's multiplier–accelerator model [P. Samuelson, 1939]. A stable multiplier–accelerator model depicts damped cycles, but economists sought a persistent cycle by modifying

Samuelson's model. J. R. Hicks and R. M. Goodwin used a nonlinear accelerator to obtain a maintained cycle [J. R. Hicks, 1950], [R. M. Goodwin, 1951].

Kitchin's cycle is the shortest one (about 40 months), and is connected with inventory investment. A typical model is due to L. A. Metzler [L. A. Metzler, 1941]. Recently chaotic dynamics has been applied to describe it [A. Medio, 1992].

Fluctuations in the 70s and 80s could not be approximated only by regular sine or cosine curves, but were also affected by politics. The first and second oil-shocks and international policy coordination are political events that were not purely domestic, but were affected by international politics. Nordhaus has modeled domestic political events in an economic model [W. D. Nordhaus, 1975].

3. Cycle Analysis of Deterministic Systems

Cycle Analysis of Single Difference Equation

Econometric models have been constructed to express such cycles. This section deals with extracting cycles from estimated econometric models. Methods for cyclical analysis of linear deterministic econometric models have been established. It should be noted that extracting cycles from a deterministic system clarifies not only the deterministic system but also the corresponding stochastic system. Deterministic cyclical analysis for a stochastic system tries to extract cycles inherent in the system, which is separated from exogenous random shocks. R. Frisch distinguished the concept of propagation problems from impulse problems [R. Frisch, 1933].

Cyclical Analysis for a single and a simultaneous difference equation system can be undertaken. For this purpose various kinds of equation form have to be distinguished.

Structural Form

$$A(L)\boldsymbol{y}_t = F\boldsymbol{z}_t + \boldsymbol{u}_t \tag{3.1}$$

$$A(L) = A_0 - A_1L - A_2L^2 - \cdots - A_mL^m$$

$$F = (F_1 \vdots F_2)$$

$$\boldsymbol{z}_t = [\boldsymbol{z}_t^{(1)'} \vdots \boldsymbol{z}_t^{(2)'}]' : \text{exogenous variables}$$

$$\boldsymbol{z}_t^{(1)} : \text{controllable policy instrument}$$

$$\boldsymbol{z}_t^{(2)} : \text{uncontrollable exogenous variables}$$

$$\boldsymbol{u}_t : \text{exogenous random shock}$$

Theil-Boot's Final Form

$$\boldsymbol{y}_t = A(L)^{-1}F\boldsymbol{z}_t + A(L)^{-1}\boldsymbol{u}_t \tag{3.2}$$

Alternative of Theil-Boot's Final Form

$$\boldsymbol{y}_t = |A(L)|^{-1}[A(L)^*F\boldsymbol{z}_t + A(L)^*\boldsymbol{u}_t] \tag{3.3}$$

$$|A(L)| : \text{determinant of } A(L)$$

$$A(L)^* : \text{adjoint of } A(L)$$

Final Autoregressive Form

$$|A(L)|\boldsymbol{y}_t = A(L)^*F\boldsymbol{z}_t + A(L)^*\boldsymbol{u}_t \tag{3.4}$$

I will select one equation from the final autoregressive form. This is to be a single autoregressive form with a non-homogeneous term and without random shocks.

$$y_t = a_1y_{t-1} + a_2y_{t-2} + \cdots + a_my_{t-m} + f_t \tag{3.5}$$

The non-homogeneous term is dependent upon time t, but is not expressed as an explicit function of t. (See Remark 1) The steady-state solution is defined to be the point to which the model value converges in the long-run, if the convergence condition holds. The long-run solution will satisfy the following equation:

$$\bar{y}_t = a_1\bar{y}_t + a_2\bar{y}_t + \cdots + a_m\bar{y}_t + f_t \tag{3.6}$$

Subtraction of (3.5) from (3.6) yields

$$(y_t - \bar{y}_t) = a_1(y_{t-1} - \bar{y}_t) + a_2(y_{t-2} - \bar{y}_t) + \cdots + a_m(y_{t-m} - \bar{y}_t)\,; \tag{3.7}$$

Therefore the solution of the autoregression of $(y_t - \bar{y}_t)$ obeys

$$y_t - \bar{y}_t = \sum_{j=1}^{L_1}(A_j \cos Q_jt + B_j \sin Q_jt)\gamma_j^t + \sum_{j=1}^{L_2} C_j\lambda_j^t \tag{3.8}$$

[H. Wold, 1954]. In a case of multiplicity of roots, coefficients A_j, B_j, C_j are expressed as a polynomial in time t: two-multiple roots takes a coefficient as a first order polynomial, and three-multiple roots one of a second order polynomial. The characteristic equation for (3.8) is

$$\lambda^m - a_1\lambda^{m-1} - a_2\lambda^{m-2} - \cdots - a_{m-1}\lambda - a_m = 0\,. \tag{3.9}$$

The first part of the solution in (3.8) corresponds to the complex roots $\gamma_j(\cos Q_j + i\sin Q_j)(j = 1, 2, \ldots, L_1)$ of the characteristic equation, and the second part to the real roots $\lambda_j(j = 1, 2, \ldots, L_2)$. Hence the relation $2L_1 + L_2 = m$ holds. The endogenous fluctuation of $(y_t - \bar{y}_t)$ in (3.9) depends on the features of characteristic roots. The dynamic properties are explained in Table 2. (Remark 2)

Table 2. Classification of roots

complex root		cycle, period $T_j = 2\pi/Q_j$
real root	$\lambda_j > 1$	explosive, non-oscillatory
	$\lambda_j = 1$	constant, non-oscillatory
	$0 \leq \lambda_j < 1$	damped, non-oscillatory
	$-1 < \lambda_j < 0$	damped, oscillatory
	$\lambda_j = -1$	constant, oscillatory
	$\lambda_j < -1$	explosive, oscillatory

One can examine the dynamic properties of endogenous fluctuation about the steady-state solution. Roots with modulus less than unity, associated with both complex and real roots, assure that solution y_t converges to $\bar{y}_t$, and it is said the system is stable. (see Remark 3)

Cycle Analysis of Simultaneous Difference Equations

The simultaneous equation system (3.1) with non-homogeneous terms but without disturbance terms is assumed to be the following:

$$A_0\boldsymbol{y}_t = A_1\boldsymbol{y}_{t-1} + A_2\boldsymbol{y}_{t-2} + \cdots + A_m\boldsymbol{y}_{t-m} + F_1\boldsymbol{z}_t^{(1)} + F_2\boldsymbol{z}_t^{(2)} \tag{3.10}$$

$\boldsymbol{y}_t$: endogenous variables

$z_t^{(1)}$: policy instrument variables

$z_t^{(2)}$: uncontrollable exogenous variables

Now let us define a steady-state solution in the same way as in the single equation by fixing the policy instrument and uncontrollable exogenous variables.

$$A_0\bar{y}_t = A_1\bar{y}_t + A_2\bar{y}_t + \cdots + A_m\bar{y}_t + F_1 z_t^{(1)} + F_2 z_t^{(2)} \tag{3.11}$$

Rearranging the terms, we get the following equation:

$$\bar{y}_t = (A_0 - A_1 - A_2 - \cdots - A_m)^{-1}(F_1 z_t^{(1)} + F_2 z_t^{(2)}) \tag{3.12}$$

The steady-state solution $\bar{y}_t$ is obviously different from the short-term equilibrium y_t. The reason why the steady-state solution is still dependent upon t is that the policy instrument and uncontrollable exogenous variables depend on t. If the system converges to the steady-state solution, the system is said to be stable. Subtraction of (3.10) from (3.11) yields the following.

$$A_0(y_t - \bar{y}_t) = A_1(y_{t-1} - \bar{y}_t) + A_2(y_{t-2} - \bar{y}_t) + \cdots + A_m(y_{t-m} - \bar{y}_t) \tag{3.13}$$

Dynamic properties of the vector autoregression $(y_t - \bar{y}_t)$ are investigated. The corresponding simultaneous characteristic equation is

$$|A_0\lambda^m - A_1\lambda^{m-1} - A_2\lambda^{m-2} - \cdots - A_{m-1}\lambda - A_m| = 0\,. \tag{3.14}$$

This form was called the "generalized eigenvalue problem" [K. Mori, 1971]. It is now possible to calculate characteristic roots of (3.14) in a direct way by the use of the definition of a determinant. Since a direct search for characteristic roots may be complicated, it is usual to transform the equation (3.14) into a first-order equation. Below, without loss of generality, we treat $A_0 = I$.

$$\begin{pmatrix} y_t \\ y_{t-1} \\ y_{t-2} \\ \vdots \\ y_{t-m+1} \end{pmatrix} = \begin{pmatrix} A_1 & A_2 & \cdots & A_{m-1} & A_m \\ I & 0 & \cdots & 0 & 0 \\ 0 & I & \cdots & 0 & 0 \\ \vdots & \vdots & \cdots & \ddots & \vdots \\ 0 & 0 & 0 & I & 0 \end{pmatrix} \begin{pmatrix} y_{t-1} \\ y_{t-2} \\ y_{t-3} \\ \vdots \\ y_{t-m} \end{pmatrix} \tag{3.15}$$

As the above equation can be expressed as $Y_t = AY_{t-1}$, the corresponding characteristic root problem is written down in the following way:

$$|A - \lambda I| = 0 \quad \text{or} \quad |\lambda I - A| = 0 \tag{3.16}$$

Now it is easy to handle the problem. The latter treatment has the drawback of big dimensionality and a possibility of accumulating errors in the computing process, while the former method does not. Characteristic roots can be shown to be the same in both approaches, theoretically.

4. Characteristics of Econometric Models in the High-Economic Growth Era — Examples with TCER and Wharton Models

Cycle Analysis for the Autoregressive Final Form of the TCER-V8 Model

A computer algorithm enables us to obtain a single autoregressive final form of GNP from the structural form. The model to be taken in this section is the TCER-V8 Model from the Tokyo Center of Economic Research (Department of Industrial Structure) [K. Mori, 1964]. The system is composed of 18 behavioral equations and 13 identities (31 equations). The sample period covers 1953 quarter IV to 1961 quarter I. The model explains the first half of the high economic growth period in the Japanese economy. As one equation is nonlinear, it is linearized. By the use of an appropriate computer algorithm, a system of 31 simultaneous equations, with 4 maximum lags in each equation, is tranformed into a 17th order autoregressive final form of GNP. It took about 15 hours of computer time in 1974.

$$\begin{aligned} GNP_t &= \sum_{i=1}^{17} \alpha_i GNP_{t-i} + \sum_{i=0}^{17}\sum_{j=1}^{3} \beta_i z^{(1)}_{t-i,j} \\ &\quad + \sum_{i=0}^{17}\sum_{j=1}^{10} \gamma_i z^{(2)}_{t-i,j} + \sum_{i=0}^{17}\sum_{j=1}^{18} \delta_i u_{t-i,j}\,. \end{aligned} \tag{4.1}$$

$z^{(1)}_{t,j} = i_t, L_{H,t}, G_{F,t}$

$z^{(2)}_{t,j} = O_t, M_W, T_R, T_G, D_G, e, t, Q_2, Q_3, Q_4$

GNP : real GNP

i : interest rate, bank loan

L_H : money supply for dwelling construction

G_F : government expenditure

O : unfilled orders of machinery

M_W : volume of world trade

T_R : government transfers

T_G : surplus of government enterprises

D_G : depreciation of government enterprises

e : statistical discrepancy

t : time trend

Q_2, Q_3, Q_4 : seasonal dummy

$u_1, \dots, u_{18}$: stochastic terms of behavioral equations

The constant term adds to -0.6193092. Detailed values of coefficients are omitted. The characteristic equation is the following.

$$\begin{aligned}\lambda^{17} &- 1.1967\lambda^{16} - 1.4588\lambda^{15} + 1.5517\lambda^{14} + 0.5327\lambda^{13} \\ &+ 0.6146\lambda^{12} - 0.5419\lambda^{11} - 1.4491\lambda^{10} + 0.5582\lambda^{9} + 0.4598\lambda^{8} \\ &+ 0.0191\lambda^{7} + 0.0560\lambda^{6} - 0.1253\lambda^{5} - 0.0417\lambda^{4} + 0.0168\lambda^{3} \\ &+ 0.0003\lambda^{2} + 0.0001\lambda - 0.0001 = 0\,. \end{aligned} \tag{4.2}$$

The characteristic roots are in Table 3.

Table 3. Characteristic Roots and Cycles of the TCER-V8 Model

real part	complex part	modulus	cycle(year)	economic cycle
1.0686		1.0686		endogenous growth
−0.995		0.995		
−0.8666		0.867		
−0.6222		0.622		
−0.565		0.565		
0.9280	±0.0963	0.933	15.19	long Juglar cycle
0.8346	±0.3918	0.922	3.572	Kitchin cycle
−0.2307	±0.8711	0.901	0.859	
−0.0708	±0.5854	0.590	0.929	
0.2160	±0.0620	0.225	5.620	short Juglar cycle
−0.0888	±0.1461	0.171	0.742	

The table is interesting. First, a real root greater than unity shows that Japanese economy in the first half of the high economic growth period has endogenous expansion of about 7% per year. The source of this endogeneity is in private fixed investment. The behavioral equation of fixed investment is

Fixed Investment

$$I_F = -773.0 + 0.543(P_C - T_C) + 0.0667(K_F)_{-1} + 0.820(P_C - T_C)_{-3} - 9.64Q_2 + 54.8Q_3 + 62.0Q_4\,. \tag{4.3}$$

$$R(\text{adj.}) = 0.992 \qquad W = 24.4 \qquad d = 2.02$$

Attention should be paid to the coefficient (+0.0667) of capital stock. Theoretically, it should be negative because of the model hypothesis of the stock adjustment principle. A positive value accounts for endogenous growth of 6.9% annually. Private fixed investment grew by 25% on average in the sample period, and shows 60% at the highest point. This is the main source of high economic growth of the Japanese economy. This investment is measured as a gross concept. It was interpreted at the time as new investment.

Second, a strong cycle of 15 years may be the Kuznets cycle in terms of periodicity although it is a bit short. Relevant equations for private residential investment merit close examination.

Private residential investment

$$I_H = -31.2 + 0.0470Y_d + 2.07(L_H)_{-2} - 0.504Q_2 - 0.562Q_3 - 20.9Q_4$$

$$R(\text{adj.}) = 0.954 \qquad W = 5.29 \qquad d = 2.13 \tag{4.4}$$

Depreciation of residential investment

$$D_H = -50.6 + 0.0120Y_d + 0.0269\{K_H + (K_H)_{-1}\}/2 - 0.341Q_2 - 1.73Q_3 - 8.46Q_4$$

$$R(\text{adj.}) = 0.966 \qquad W = 2.53 \qquad d = 0.569 \tag{4.5}$$

Stock of residences

$$K_H = I_H - D_H + (K_H)_{-1}\,. \tag{4.6}$$

As money supply for residential investment L_H is exogenous, it has nothing to do with the generation of a cycle. Since household disposable income Y_d is a current value, it cannot make cycles. Depreciation and residential capital stock interact with a lag, but they never affect income-related variables, and cannot make cycles. The cycle of 15 years seems to be made from other mechanisms.

Let us look at fixed investment again.

Private fixed investment

$$I_F = -773.0 + 0.543(P_C - T_C) + 0.0667(K_F)_{-1} + 0.820(P_C - T_C)_{-3} - 9.64Q_2 + 54.8Q_3 + 62.0Q_4 \tag{4.7}$$

$R(\text{adj.}) = 0.992 \qquad W = 24.4 \qquad d = 2.02$

$P_C - T_C$: corporate profit less corporate tax

Depreciation of fixed investment

$$D_F = -388.0 + 0.0392\{K_F + (K_F)_{-1}\}/2 - 8.63Q_2 + 15.6Q_3 + 42.0Q_4$$

$R(\text{adj.}) = 0.991 \qquad W = 8.86 \qquad d = 1.72 \qquad (4.8)$

Capital stock

$$K_F = I_F - D_F + K_{F-1}\,. \tag{4.9}$$

As fixed investment and corporate profit interrelate with a maximum lag of 3 quarters, there is a possibility of generating cycles. Fixed investment could make two kinds of Juglar cycle: a longer one of 15 years and a shorter one of 5.6 years. Hence the fixed investment equation produces endogenous growth and two kinds of cycles in the Japanese economy.

A strong cycle of 3.5 years is a so-called 42 months Kitchin cycle (3.572 years = 42.864 months). To analyze this, we examine the relevant equations.

Inventory stock

$$K_J = 977.0 + 1.65Av(GNP^*) + 0.950(O)_{-1} - 211.0(i)_{-1} + 54.3Q_2 - 14.7Q_3 + 84.1Q_4 \tag{4.10}$$

$R(\text{adj.}) = 0.995 \qquad W = 101.0 \qquad d = 1.36$

$Av(GNP^*) : (GNP^*_{-1} + GNP^*_{-2} + GNP^*_{-3} + GNP^*_{-4})/4$

GNP^* : GNP of private sector

O : unfilled orders of machinery

i : interest rate

Inventory investment

$$J = K_J - (K_J)_{-1} \,. \tag{4.11}$$

Since unfilled orders of machinery (O) and the interest rate (i) are exogenous, they are not responsible for endogenous cycles. GNP of the private sector and inventory stock will interact to make cycles.

We have shown that we can observe typical cycles by the roots extracted from an estimated TCER model. The system is unstable because it has endogenous growth. However, the deviations from trend growth are stable.

Cycle Analysis of the Wharton Model

Although the two methods of cycle extraction in simultaneous equation systems must theoretically have the same roots, different sets of roots have been reported in numerical analysis of the Wharton model in 45-equation condensed version [B. Hickman, 1972]. E. P. Howrey transformed the nonlinear large scale Wharton model into a linear system of 45 equations. Howrey computed 17 real roots, while Mori found 15 roots. (see Table 4)

Table 4. Real Roots of the Condensed Version of the Wharton Model

Mori	Howrey	Mori	Howrey
1.0044	1.0047	0.6249	0.6217
1.0000	1.0000	0.4746	0.4918
	0.9619	0.1823	0.1887
0.9452	0.9448	−0.3559	−0.3291
0.8779	0.8779	−0.4601	−0.4583
	0.8651	−0.5503	−0.5504
0.8307	0.8375	−0.6084	−0.6086
0.7725	0.7663	−0.8112	−0.8500
0.7428	0.7404		

Although the two computing methods produce nearly the same roots, Mori's method has no real roots of 0.9619 and 0.8651. What is interesting is both methods extract an endogenous growth factor of about 0.4% (1.004), and they have real roots of unity.

Next Table 5 shows complex roots. Whereas Mori has 14 pairs of complex roots, Howrey has 13. 12 pairs are approximately the same; Mori's first two pairs, and Howrey's last pair differ. Mori's first two pairs have cycles of 27 quarters (6.77 years) and 59 quarters (14.72 years), respectively with modulus 0.84 and 0.83 (strong power). However Howrey's last complex root has a cycle of 96 quarters (24 years) causing divergence. Howrey's last root is doubtful, for its corresponding determinant does not vanish.

What is interesting for us in comparing both models (Japan and USA) are their common features. (see Table 6)

Table 5. Complex Roots of the Condensed Version of the Wharton Model

Mori				Howrey			
real part	complex part	modulus	period	real part	complex part	modulus	period
0.8190	0.1934	0.8415	6.7743				
0.8249	0.0884	0.8296	14.720				
−0.0855	0.6531	0.6587	0.9234	−0.0903	0.6566	0.6628	0.9199
−0.0820	0.6418	0.6470	0.9252	−0.0843	0.6141	0.6199	0.9201
−0.0619	0.6129	0.6161	0.9398	−0.0621	0.6117	0.6148	0.9395
−0.0662	0.5776	0.5814	0.9323	−0.0672	0.5780	0.5819	0.9313
−0.0496	0.4800	0.4825	0.9385	−0.0498	0.4788	0.4814	0.9381
−0.0548	0.5519	0.5546	0.9407	−0.0517	0.5527	0.5551	0.9439
−0.0612	0.5516	0.5550	0.9343	−0.0609	0.5497	0.5531	0.9343
−0.5865	0.0096	0.5866	0.5026	−0.5858	0.0104	0.5859	0.5029
−0.5232	0.0026	0.5232	0.5008	−0.5221	0.0032	0.5221	0.5010
−0.1316	0.1348	0.1884	0.6701	−0.1429	0.1485	0.2061	0.6721
0.0651	0.1317	0.1469	1.4129	0.0808	0.1356	0.1579	1.5196
−0.0013	0.0200	0.0200	0.9588	−0.0012	0.0200	0.0200	0.9622
				1.1344	0.0743	1.1368	24.007

Table 6. Cycles of TCER and Wharton Models

TCER Cycles	Wharton Cycles (Mori)
1.0689	1.0044
	1.0000
15.19(0.933)	14.720(0.8296)
5.620(0.225)	6.7743(0.8415)
3.572(0.922)	

Stability and Instability Properties of Historical Econometric Models

In the final section I investigate stability and instability properties of some historical econometric models, by dividing recent history, beginning from the end of the World War I, into three eras: (1) interwar era and the World War II including the Great Depression (20s–40s), (2) high economic growth era (50s–60s), (3) unstable era (70s–80s). Among the divisions we have the end of World War II and the end of the Vietnam War. The two models already analyzed have been constructed to describe both the US and Japanese economies in the high economic growth era. For comparing cyclical behavior between the interwar era and the high economic growth era, I will take Klein's Model I and the Klein–Goldberger Model for reference [L. R. Klein, 1950], [A. S. Goldberger, 1959]. Table 7 and Table 8 show dynamic properties of both models, which turn out to be stable.

Table 7. Characteristic Roots and Periods of Klein Model I

	OLS	2SLS	LIML	3SLS
real root	0.3554	0.2975	0.2940	0.3435
complex root	0.6783	0.7701	0.7843	0.7785
	±0.4017i	±0.3492i	±0.3164i	±0.3914i
modulus	0.7884	0.8456	0.8458	0.8714
period	11.7508	14.7511	16.3921	13.4909
up-crossings	5.9122	6.5718	6.1326	7.1799
spectral peak	9.0492	12.4328	14.8462	12.2552

Table 8. Characteristic Roots of KG Model

tax:exogenous	modulus	period	tax:endogenous	modulus	period
Goldberger calculation (real condensed system)					
0.9527	0.9527		0.8468	0.8468	
0.1760	0.1760		0.4595	0.4595	
$0.4800 \pm 0.2483i$	0.5404	13.16	$0.1887 \pm 0.2353i$	0.3016	7.02
Howrey calculation (whole system, roots larger than 0.05)					
0.9815	0.9815		0.9941	0.9941	
0.8162	0.8162		0.9815	0.9815	
0.6145	0.6145		0.9776	0.9776	
0.3211	0.3211		0.8483	0.8483	
−0.0762	0.0762		0.8139	0.8139	
			0.3321	0.3321	
			−0.0811	0.0811	
$0.9813 \pm 0.0104i$	0.9814	592.9	$0.6046 \pm 0.0396i$	0.6059	96.1
$0.8504 \pm 0.2239i$	0.8794	24.4	0.1076 ± 0.2395	0.2626	5.5
$0.2329 \pm 0.2063i$	0.3119	8.7			

Now I will characterize historical econometric models keeping in mind the three divisions of economic eras in the light of stability properties of the estimated econometric models. (see Table 9)

The interwar era has highly stable models. Stochastic properties were analysed by P. Dhrymes using the argument of stationary stochastic process [P. J. Dhrymes, 1970]. The stability of models in the interwar era seems to come from weak power of the capitalist economy, which was probably caused by a deficiency of fixed investment and of innovation. In this era, since human and economic resources were devoted to executing war, economic power was probably reduced.

The high economic growth era produces an unstable model in that a real root is greater than unity. Stochastic properties were analyzed by G. C. Chow [G. C.Chow, 1975]. The instability of models in the high economic growth era stemmed from the fact that capitalist economies were full of power.

However, in the third unstable era, researchers have not taken interest in this kind of cycle analysis. The models are likely to have a unit root, which produces a trend. Econometric researchers have recently been involved in statistical testing for unit roots. Unfortunately we do not have cyclical stochastic properties for ARIMA models. And the probable instability of models in the unstable era may result from a mechanism of hyperinflation on the one hand (root greater than unity), and instability of the financial sector, as Minsky has indicated (unit root instability) on the other hand [H. P. Minsky, 1986].

Table 9. Characteristics of Historical Econometric Models

Era	Interwar Era	High Economic Growth Era	Unstable Era
	20s·30s·40s	50s·60s	70s·80s
example	Klein Model I 1921–1941 K·G Model 1929–1952	TCER Model 1953.4–1961.1 Wharton Model 1948.1–1965.4	
roots	$\|\lambda\| < 1$ stable	$\lambda_{\text{real}} > 1$ unstable	$\lambda_{\text{real}} > 1$? $\lambda_{\text{real}} = 1$? unstable
	[P. J. Dhrymes, 1970]	[G. C. Chow, 1975]	statistical test for unit root ARIMA

References

1. G. C. Chow, *Analysis and Control of Dynamic Economic Systems* (John Wiley & Sons, New York, 1975).
2. P. J. Dhrymes, *Econometrics, Statistical Foundations and Applications* (Harper and Row, New York, 1970).
3. P. J. Dhrymes, *Mathematics for Econometrics* (Springer-Verlag, New York, 1978).
4. G. S. Fishman, *Spectral Methods in Econometrics* (Holden-Day, San Francisco, 1969).
5. R. Frisch, "Propagation problems and impulse problems in dynamic economics," in *Essays in Honour of Gustav Cassel* (George Allen & Unwin, London, 1933).
6. A. S. Goldberger, *Impact Multipliers and Dynamic Properties of the Klein–Goldberger Model* (North-Holland, Amsterdam, 1959).

7. R. M. Goodwin, "The nonlinear accelerator and the persistence of business cycles," *Econometrica*, vol. **29**, pp. 1–18 (1951).
8. R. M. Goodwin, *Chaotic Economic Dynamics* (Oxford University Press, Oxford, 1990).
9. B. Hickman (ed.), *Econometric Models of Cyclical Behavior, vol. 1 & vol. 2* (Columbia University Press, New York, 1972).
10. J. R. Hicks, *A Contribution to the Theory of the Trade Cycle*n (Oxford University Press, Oxford, 1950).
11. K. Inada & H. Uzawa, *Economic Development and Fluctuations* (Iwanami, Tokyo, 1972).
12. W. G. Kelly & A. C. Peterson, *Difference Equations* (Academic Press, Boston, 1991).
13. L. R. Klein, *Economic Fluctuations in the United States, 1921–1941*, Cowles Commission Monograph **11** (John Wiley and Sons, New York, 1950).
14. A. Medio, *Chaotic Dynamics* (Cambridge University Press, Cambridge, 1992).
15. L. A. Metzler, "The nature and stability of inventory cycles", *Review of Economic Statistics*, vol. **XXIII**, pp. 113–129 (1941).
16. H. P. Minsky, *Stabilizing an Unstable Economy* (Yale University Press, New Haven, 1986).
17. K. Mori, "Simulation analysis of growth and fluctuation in the postwar Japanese Economy: 1955–1960," in ed. R. Komiya, *Economic Growth in Postwar Japan* (Iwanami, Tokyo, 1964), (in Japanese).
18. K. Mori, "Generalized eigenvalue problem of econometric models," *Econometrica*, vol. **39**, no. 4, pp. 193–195 (1971).
19. W. D. Nordhaus, "The political business cycle," *Review of Economic Studies*, vol. **42**, no. 130, pp. 169–90 (1975).
20. P. A. Samuelson, "Interaction between the multiplier analysis and the principle of acceleration," *Review of Economic Statistics*, vol. **21**, pp. 75–78 (1939).
21. J. A. Schumpeter, *Business Cycles: A Theoretical Historical, and Statistical Analysis of the Capitalist Process* (McGraw-Hill, New York, 1939).
22. M. Shinohara, "Growth and fluctuations", in *Economic Dictionary I* (Toyokeizai, Tokyo, 1980), (in Japanese).
23. A. Tanaka, *World System* (University of Tokyo Press, Tokyo, 1989), (in Japanese).
24. H. Wold, *A Study in the Analysis of Stationary Time Series* (Almqvist and Wicksell, Uppsala, 1954).

Remark 1: The case in which the non-homogeneous term is expressed as a function of time t is treated in P. Dhrymes and W. G. Kelly.
P. J. Dhrymes, *Mathematics for Econometrics* (Springer-Verlag, New York, 1978), chapter 5;
W. G. Kelly & A. C. Peterson, *Difference Equations* (Academic Press, Boston, 1991), chapter 3.

The former obtains a special solution by the use of the lag operator, and the latter by the annihilator method. The general solution is the sum of the particular solution and general solution of corresponding homogeneous equation.

Remark 2: The autoregressive final form is estimated, and the coefficients are subject to sample fluctuation.

A. T. Bharucha-Reid & M. Sambandham, *Random Polynomials* (Academic Press, New York, 1986).

Remark 3: The investigation of stability of difference equation by the Lyapunov qualitative theory is new.

V. Lakshmikantham & D. Trigiante, *Theory of Difference Equations: Numerical Methods and Applications* (Academic Press, New York, 1988).

COMMENTS ON HIROYUKI KOSAKA'S "DYNAMIC PROPERTIES OF TCER AND RELATED MODELS"

TAKU YAMAMOTO
Department of Economics
Hitotsubashi University

Professor Kosaka's paper is an interesting review of business cycle theory based upon econometric models. He concentrates mostly on the deterministic cycles derived from the characteristic roots of models, in particular those of the TCER model and the Wharton model. As for the TCER model, he also attempts to find a sector which can be a cause of a particular cycle. I will make three technical comments on his paper. My comments are not necessarily to criticize his paper, but rather to supplement it.

1. Interpretation of Cycles Based upon Characteristic Roots

In Sec. 4, Professor Kosaka discusses cyclical behavior mostly in terms of deterministic cycles, that is, the cycles implied by the characteristic roots of the model. I will discuss an alternative aspect of cyclical behavior based upon econometric models. The argument here is not original but well-known. A more detailed account is given in Professor Klein's paper in this volume, and also can be found in his books (1971, 1974, Chap. 6)

(a) *Deterministic Cycles*

For illustrative purposes, let us consider the following second order homogeneous difference equation:

$$y_t + ay_{t-1} + by_{t-2} = 0 \qquad (t = 1, 2, \ldots, T),$$

where a and b are parameters. Suppose that the roots of the model are complex, since we do not have interesting deterministic cycles when they are real. They are given by

$$\lambda_1\,,\,\lambda_2 = \rho(\cos\theta \pm i\sin\theta)\,,$$

where $\theta = \cos^{-1}\{-a/(2\sqrt{b})\}$ and $\rho = \sqrt{b}$. The so-called deterministic cycle is described by θ, which is the frequency in radians. The period of the cycle is given by $2\pi/\theta$.

The solution of the model is given by

$$y_t = A\rho^t(\cos\theta t + \gamma)\,,$$

where A and γ are appropriately determined by the initial values, say y_{-1} and y_0. From the above, it is easily seen that, when $|\rho| < 1$, the solution converges to 0 as t increases. See Fig. 1 for a sample series of the deterministic solution for $\rho = 0.8$ and $\theta = \pi/4$. When $|\rho| > 1$, the solution explodes. Only when $\rho = 1$, does the solution exhibit a sustained cycle with a period of $2\pi/\theta$. See Fig. 2 for a sample series of the deterministic solution for $\rho = 1.0$ and $\theta = \pi/4$. Thus, it appears rather difficult to attribute the sustained cycle to the deterministic cycle.

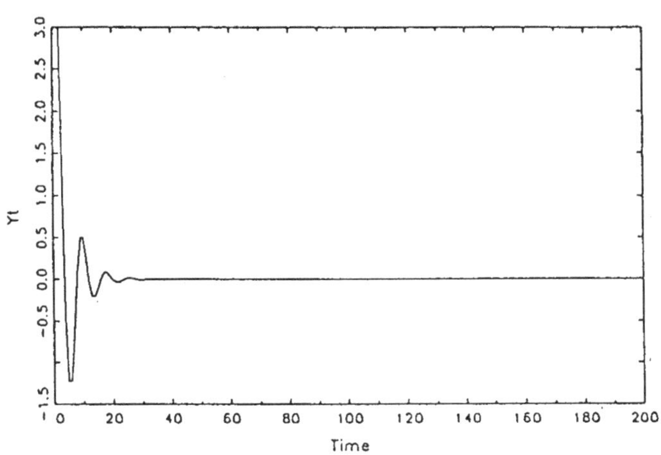

Fig. 1. Deterministic Solution: $y_t = 1.1313y_{t-1} - 0.64y_{t-2} + u_t$ ($\rho = 0.8$ and $\theta = \pi/4$).

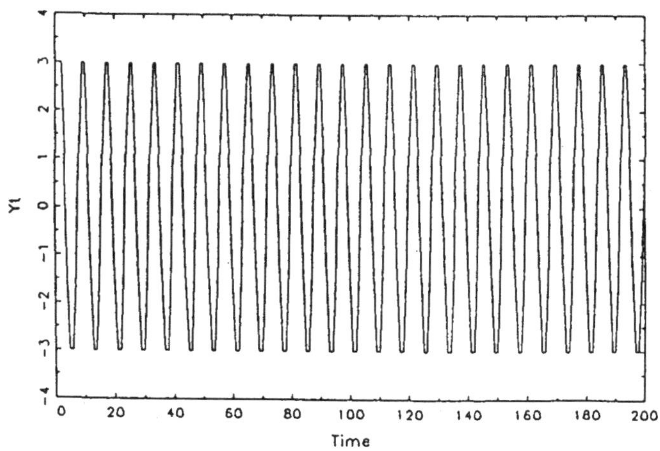

Fig. 2. Deterministic Solution: $y_t = 1.4142 y_{t-1} - 1.0 y_{t-2} + u_t$ ($\rho = 1.0$ and $\theta = \pi/4$).

(b) *Stochastic Cycles*

We now consider the stochastic difference equation which includes an error term.

$$y_t + a y_{t-1} + b y_{t-2} = u_t \,,$$

where a and b are parameters and $\{u_t\}$ is white noise. The characteristic roots of the model are the same as before. The solution of the above model is generalized as

$$y_t = A\rho^t(\cos\theta t + \gamma) + (\lambda_1 - \lambda_2)^{-1} \sum_{i=0}^{t-1} \left(\lambda_1^{i+1} - \lambda_2^{i+1}\right) u_{t-i} \,.$$

Thus, the solution consists of two terms; that is, the deterministic part and the stochastic part. When $|\rho| > 1$, the solution explodes. When $|\rho| = 1$, it is known that the stochastic solution explodes, although the deterministic solution exhibits a sustained cycle. See Fig. 4 for a sample series of the stochastic solution for $\rho = 1.0$ and $\theta = \pi/4$. Obviously, the explosive solution is not a suitable one for the economic system. When $|\rho| < 1$, the first term vanishes as was explained above. However in this case, we can observe a sustained cycle due to the second term in the above equation, although it is not as regular as the deterministic cycle. It is called the stochastic cycle. See Fig. 3 for a sample series of the stochastic solution for $\rho = 0.8$ and $\theta = \pi/4$. The frequency of the stochastic cycle is usually defined as the one at the peak in the power spectrum of the process, which is given as

$$\theta^* = \cos^{-1}\{\, -a(1+b)/(4b)\,\}\,.$$

Generally θ^* is different from θ. That is, the stochastic cycle is generally different from the deterministic cycle. The analysis of an econometric model based upon the spectral peak is given, for example, in Howrey (1971).

Furthermore, let us consider the following stochastic difference equation.

$$y_t = 0.7y_{t-1} + u_t\,.$$

The characteristic root of this model is 0.7, that is, real and not complex. The deterministic solution and its spectral analysis do not give a cycle. However, the stochastic solution of this model exhibits a sustained cycle as shown in Fig. 5. In this case, the period of the cycle may be estimated by the mean distance between up-crosses or the mean distance between peaks.

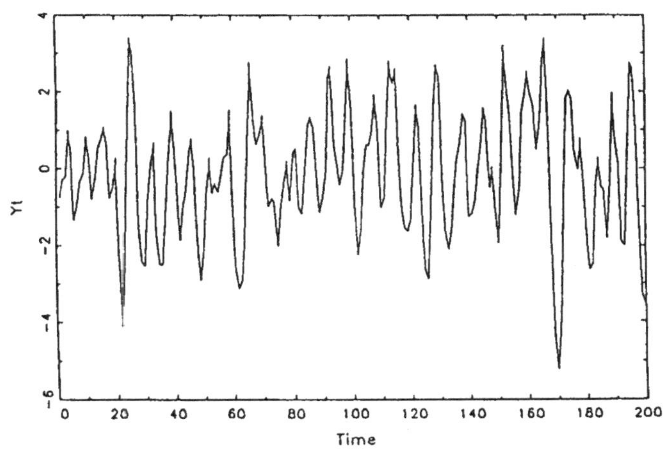

Fig. 3. Stochastic Solution: $y_t = 1.1313y_{t-1} - 0.64y_{t-2} + u_t$ ($\rho = 0.8$ and $\theta = \pi/4$).

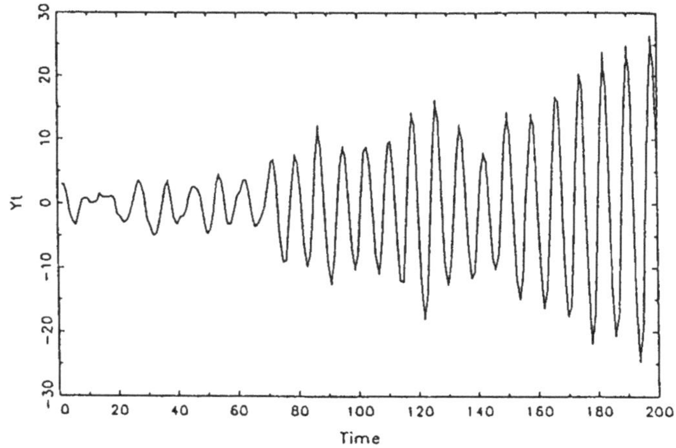

Fig. 4. Stochastic Solution: $y_t = 1.4142y_{t-1} - 1.0y_{t-2} + u_t$ ($\rho = 1.0$ and $\theta = \pi/4$).

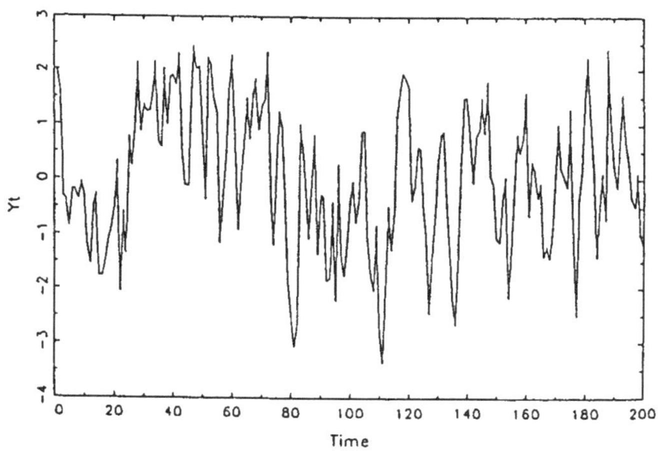

Fig. 5. Stochastic Solution: $y_t = 0.7y_{t-1} + u_t$ ($\rho = 0.7$ and $\theta = 0$).

In conclusion, the stochastic solution with $|\rho| < 1$ allows for a rich variety of sustained cycles. And it may be more appropriate to interpret the observed cycles in terms of stochastic cycles rather than deterministic cycles.

2. Downward bias of Estimates of Characteristic Roots When Trend Variables are Included in the Regression Model

Professor Kosaka argues that the interwar US economy is stable because all the characteristic roots are distinctively less than unity in absolute value, based upon Howrey's work (1971). In what follows, I argue that characteristic roots are estimated with downward bias in small samples. It has been known that the OLS estimates of a non-stationary model are strongly biased downward. See, for example, the critical values reported in Fuller (1976, Chap. 8) for the test of a unit root. The following two Monte Carlo Experiments show how large the bias is in a small sample.

First, let the true model be explosive, as follows:

$$y_t = 1.05y_{t-1} + u_t\,, \qquad (t = 1, 2, \ldots, T)$$

where u_t is independently identically distributed as $N(0,1)$. I estimated the following regression model to the data generated from the above model.

$$y_t = \alpha + \beta y_{t-1} + \gamma t + u_t$$

The number of replications is 500. The mean and variance of 500 OLS estimates of β are given in Table 1. As seen in the table, the OLS estimate of β is strongly biased downward when the sample size is small, say $T = 50$.

Table 1. Mean and Variance of $\hat{\beta}$

T	50	100	500
Mean	0.917	1.041	1.050
Variance	0.120	0.034	0.001

For the second experiment, let the true model be a random walk with drift:

$$y_t = 1 + y_{t-1} + u_t\,.$$

I estimated the same regression model as above to the data. The number of replications is also 500. The mean and variance of 500 OLS estimates of β are given in Table 2. As seen from the table, we get a similar downward bias as in the first experiment.

Table 2. Mean and Variance of $\hat{\beta}$

T	50	100	500
Mean	0.817	0.907	0.980
Variance	0.106	0.054	0.012

These experiments show that when the sample size is small, there exists a high possibility of downward bias in the estimate of β. The model discussed by Professor Kosaka, that is, Klein Model I, was estimated with a very small sample size and the trend variable was included as an explanatory variable. Thus, while Professor Kosaka argues that most characteristic roots are distinctively less than unity in modulus for the interwar period, we should be careful to state that the system was stable in that period.

3. Is It Possible to Attribute a Cycle to a Particular Equation?

When discussing the final form of TCER-V8 Model, Professor Kosaka attributes each important type of cycle to some particular sector or equation. However, the model is not block-diagonal or block-triangular, and the final form is jointly determined by all the equations in the system. Thus, his argument does not allow for the multiplicity of sources of cycle types.

References

1. W. A. Fuller, *Introduction to Statistical Time Series* (John Wiley and Sons, New York, 1976).
2. E. P. Howrey, "Dynamic Properties of the Klein-Goldberger Model", *Econometrica*, **39**, 73–87 (1971) .
3. L. R. Klein, *An Essay on the Theory of Economic Prediction* (Markham Publishing Co., Chicago, 1971).
4. L. R. Klein, *Textbook of Econometrics, 2nd. ed.* (Prentice-Hall, New Jersey, 1974).

A MODEL OF GROWTH RATE CYCLES AND THE RESONANCE/DOUBLE-CLUTCH EFFECT OF PUBLIC INVESTMENT

FUMIMASA HAMADA

Rm. 401, Department of Economics, Tokyo International University
1-13-1 Matoba-Kita, Kawagoe-shi 350-11, Japan

1. Introduction

When we observe actual business cycles, two major factors can be considered for generating them; one is the endogenous cycle as a structural characteristic of the economy in question, and the other is the cycle caused by changes in some exogenous factors such as macroeconomic policy instruments, exchange rates, and so forth. Among exogenous factors, the role of macroeconomic policy instruments seems to be very important in analyzing the cyclical behavior of the Japanese economy in its relation to effectiveness of such policy instruments.

In any country, macroeconomic policy should be specific in order to reflect the national characteristics in its execution. The past experiences of the economic fluctuations in Japan, particularly after the first oil crisis, tells us that the government, facing a turning point from boom to recession, hardly changes its policy in recognition of the economic situation. It adopts an obstinate attitude about its policy stance in spite of indications of a change in business tendencies, such as successive reports of less than 50% in the business-cycles diffusion index.

When public recognition about change in the present state of the economy turns out to be significant, the Diet opens an investigation of the matter, and starts to discuss the use of possible instruments of macroeconomic policy and preparation of a supplementary budget. The government finally decides on a revised budget, and submits it to the Diet. So, just prior to the final determination of a supplementary budget, the public may change their expectations about future trends of the macroeconomy, and raise the marginal propensity to consume, raise the marginal efficiency of investment, and change the portfolio composition of their financial assets. This may be regarded as the first stage of public reaction (the reaction for the preparation of policy instruments). The second stage reaction (the reaction after the policy execution) starts as a reaction of the public to an actual increase in government expenditures. I named the total effect the "Double-Clutch" effect, like the F-1 clutch manipulation.

The Double-Clutch functioning has a quite different effect on an economy from that of the rational expectations. While reaction of the public with rational expectations is, in general, smoothed in relation to exogenous impacts like a change in government expenditures, reaction of the public with the double-clutch accelerates in response to the same types of impact, when the economy fluctuates in resonance with changes in exogenous expenditures. In an economy where the double-clutch always works effectively, the amplitude and the period of business cycles may turn out to be large.

If the government can decide on the timing of policy preparation so as to prevent an economy from getting into recession, and induce the first stage reaction of the public, and if it can also realize the corresponding policy execution, the effectiveness of macroeconomic policy will be enhanced above that expected or planned. If the government fails to do this, it will lose credibility in the eyes of the public about macroeconomic policy, so much so that the policy effect will be too small to stimulate effective demand. The timing of policy execution is therefore of utmost importance.

This paper attempts to analyze the double-clutch effect of government investment on the Japanese economy during the period from 1958 through 1990, using a quarterly model of economic growth rate cycles. A single ordinary difference equation with respect to the economic growth rate accompanying the double-clutch effect of government investment is specified. As a special case of its non-homogeneous term with the resonance effect that was analyzed theoretically by [Allen, 1956] and [Hicks, 1950], the double-clutch effect of government investment is developed, and applied to the observation period.[a]

It was concluded that although the double-clutch effect was clear for the period before the first oil crisis, this effect was hardly observed for the periods

[a] Mori(1967/1993) attempted to extract the resonance effect of the market interest rate, which is controlled by the monetary authority of Japan, using his macroeconometric model for the period of Japan's high economic growth rate. This attempt was satisfactory.

after the first oil crisis. This implies that the timing of policy preparation and excution was not appropriate in the latter period.

In the next section, a model of growth rate cycles of a macroeconomy is specified, and in Sec. 3, an equation to explain the double-clutch effect of macroeconomic policy is deduced. Section 4 presents an estimation of this model for the period 1958–90, and Sec. 5 extracts the double-clutch and resonance effect of government investment for this period.

2. A Model of Growth Rate Cycles

Many theoretical models of business cycles have so far been presented, since the non-linear accelerator models of [Hicks, 1950] and [Goodwin, 1951]. In the case where the purpose is to analyze the performance of a macroeconomy in terms of its internal structural interdependence, equations for economic behavior by sectors included in the model should be specified explicitly. Cyclical characteristics of the model may be analyzed by a dynamic solution of this model. If the sole purpose is to analyze the dynamic properties of an economy, a simpler method of study may be possible for obtaining some meaningful findings.

Nobody knows what the true structure of a macroeconomy is. There may be a unique relationship between a system of structural equations and its reduced form. The reduced-form equations transform true values of structural parameters which characterize and reflect the model's structural characteristics.

The reduced form or dynamic solution of the model for real output has a specific dynamic form, and the corresponding equation for economic growth rate could be obtained. If an appropriate form of this equation can be obtained by fitting it directly to time series data on economic growth rate, this may be considered as one of the candidates for the actual reduced form for the economic growth rate during the observation period.

It goes without saying that this reduced-form equation provides nothing more than the structural information about the cyclical characteristics of the economy in question, and it is this that is required in this study.[b] An entire process in which government investment stimulates effective demand of an economy, reduces the rate of unemployment, raises the marginal propensity

[b] The author does not know any example of a direct estimate of this type of model of cyclical behavior of a macroeconomy. [Mori, 1967/1993] has tried to estimate a linear difference equation with respect to the level of real GNP, but not of the economic growth rate.

to consume, and, therefore, increases consumption and investment, will be assumed implicitly in the model.[c] Once a tentative study has found some meaningful results, a more intensive study of the economy's cyclical behavior should be done, based on an explicit structure of the model, as attempted in [Mori, 1967/1993].

Based on the considerations described above, a single equation for the economic growth rate, as a reduced form of the model implicitly assumed to include a system of structural equations, can be specified as below:

$$y(t) = a_0 + a_1 y(t-1) + a_2 y(t-2) + \cdots + bx^*(t) + u(t)\,, \qquad (1)$$

where $y(t)$ is the real economic growth rate at period t, $x^*(t)$ is a column vector, the elements of which are the policy variables in the near future, the present and the past, in terms of growth rates. b is a row vector for the corresponding coefficients of $x^*(t)$, and $u(t)$ is a random variable with zero mean, constant variance, and no serial correlation. (1) is a linear difference equation with non-homogeneous terms, $bx^*(t)$ and $u(t)$.

The non-homogeneous terms are supposed to stimulate the cyclical fluctuations of economic growth rate through external impacts, such as changes in policy variables and random disturbances.

Suppose that there is only one policy variable which has an effective influence on the fluctuations of the economic growth rate, and that the public knows about the policy execution in advance. The non-homogeneous terms include the values of this variable in the near future, at present and in the past, so that $bx^*(t)$ can be specified as below:

$$bx^*(t) = c\{b_0 x(t+1) + b_1 x(t) + b_2 x(t-1) + b_3 x(t-2) + \dots\}\,, \qquad (2)$$

where the coefficient b_0 is a weight of the policy effect in the first (consideration and/or preparation) stage, and b_1, b_2, $b_3, \dots$ are the respective weights of the policy effects in the second (execution) stage on the economic growth rate.

This specification is different from that of the so-called "rational expectations" model in that the former restricts the availability of information on the future of the economy in question to that of the macroeconomic policy of the government, while the latter allows it to all of the endogenous and exogenous variables. Though the time path of government investment in the near future

[c]See [Hamada, 1988].

is, as a matter of fact, considered to be sometimes resonant with economic fluctuations, the explicit structure of the latter is not introduced here at all.

The cyclical structure of a macroeconomy explained by (1) can be shown explicitly with its dynamic solution for the homogeneous part of Eq. (1). The solution can be expressed by a sinusoidal function as below:

$$y^*(t) = A_0\rho_0^t + A_1\rho_1^t \cos(\theta_1 t + \omega_1) + A_2\rho_2^t \cos(\theta_2 t + \omega_2)\,, \tag{3}$$

where A, ρ, θ and ω are constant. The period of cycles T_i is $(2\pi/\theta_i)$, and the phase is ω_i, its timing τ_i is (ω_i/θ_i).

Changes in non-homogeneous terms give impacts on the cyclical variation of the economy in question which is autonomous, and consequently, economic fluctuations can be generated and compared with observed data. If Eq. (1) is estimated using reported data on relevant variables, it may be possible to make cyclical structure of the actual economy clear, and to learn something more about the effects of macroeconomic policy on the economy.

3. The Double-Clutch Effect of Government Investment

The non-homogeneous term in Eq. (1) may possibly produce the resonance phenomenon of the Allen/Hicks type, through its interactions with endogenous cycles. Aside from the resonance effect, it adds one more impact on behavior of the public who expect a change in autonomous expenditures to be brought about. It seems quite important to inquire how this combination influences actual business cycles. Suppose there is only one policy instrument which is effective to stimulate total demand, and its pattern of changes can be expressed by a sinusoidal function as below:

$$x(t) = B_0\xi_0^t + B_1\xi_1^t \cos(\lambda_1 t + \sigma_1) + B_2\xi_2^t \cos(\lambda_2 t + \sigma_2)\,, \tag{4}$$

where B, ξ, λ and σ are constants. ξ is the amplitude by which the value of the policy variable fluctuates, this fluctuation is explosive, of a regular oscillation of constant amplitude, or damped depending on $\xi > 1$, $\xi = 1$ or $\xi < 1$ respectively. The period of oscillation T is $(2\pi/\lambda)$. σ gives the value of initial location where this sinusoidal oscillation starts, the phase, and its timing τ_j is (σ_j/λ_j).

Then, if the policy variable included in the non-homogeneous term has oscillatory characteristics as shown in (4), what type of oscillatory characteristic does the economy as described by Eq. (1) have? Let us rewrite Eq. (1) as below:

$$A(L)y(t) = bx^*(t) + u(t)\,, \tag{1'}$$

where $A(L)$ is a lag polynomial. A particular solution for Eq. (2) can be written, using (4), as below:

$$bx^*(t) = C_0\xi_0^t + C_1\xi_1^t\cos(\lambda_1 t + \sigma_1) + C_2\xi_2^t\cos(\lambda_2 t + \sigma_2)\,,$$

where

$$\begin{aligned} C_1 &= \alpha B_1[b_0\xi_1\cos(\lambda_1) + b_1 + b_2/\{\xi_1\cos(\lambda_1)\} + b_3/\{\xi_1\cos(\lambda_1)\}^2 \\ C_2 &= \alpha B_2[b_0\xi_2\cos(\lambda_2) + b_1 + b_2/\{\xi_2\cos(\lambda_2)\} + b_3/\{\xi_2\cos(\lambda_2)\}^2\,, \end{aligned} \tag{5}$$

where α is a constant.

The solution of the homogeneous Eq. (3) gives a general solution for (1)′ together with solution (5). As is easily seen, the sum of these two solutions may amplify or offset one another, and which one dominates depends strongly on the phase of both solutions, the values of ω and σ. If the difference between these two values is just equal to π, or if the cyclical oscillations generated by these two solutions will completely offset each other, there will be no oscillatory fluctuation at all. On the contrary, if the phase difference between the two is not equal to π, an oscillatory fluctuation will be generated.

When the government executes a macroeconomic policy, if its impact has the same oscillatory characteristics as these endogenous cycles of the economy, the economy may react with an enlarged amplitude of oscillation. This is the resonance effect by [Allen, 1956] and [Hicks, 1950], and first tested for the period of "High Economic Growth" of the Postwar Japan by [Mori, 1967/1993]. The Double-Clutch effect is a further extension of the resonance effect by introducing a sort of announcement effect of macroeconomic policy.

If the government executes a macroeconomic policy so as to synchronize the realization of expenditures, period to period, with the endogenous path of total demand, the macroeconomy will over-react to this impact. In Fig. 1, a simple case for the government investment where the double-clutch effect works, is shown. In this figure, government investment is a_o at period 0, when this economy is in recession, and expectations of the public are pessimistic. In order to stimulate effective demand, the government and the Diet decide on an additional budget, and the execution of an increase in government investment is at the preparatory stage (*the first stage*), but it always takes some time to implement.

Suppose that the public knows, in advance, that this will be realized at period 1. Then, expectations of the public turn out to be rather optimistic, so that marginal propensity to consume and marginal efficiency of investment will rise sooner or later, before an increase in government investment actually takes place. Because of this, effective demand will begin to increase. The part of bold curve *cd* shows this process of reaction of the economy. When an increase in government investment actually takes place at period 1, this process will be accelerated, and a large scale oscillatory movement of real output will be generated, as the curve *defg* shows. The period after period 1 is the stage of execution (*the second stage*).

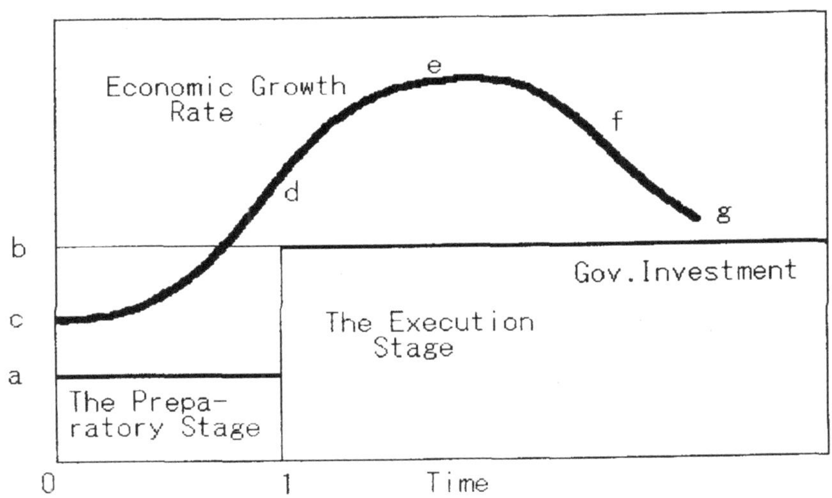

Fig. 1. The double-clutch effect of gov. investment.

Needless to say, this over-reaction of the economy is due to the sum of the first and second stage effects of macroeconomic policy on behavior of the public; that is the double-clutch effect. If the government cleverly makes use of this effect, and if it can choose timing that is appropriate to switch from the first stage to the second stage, it can attain the maximum effect with the given budget. If the first stage is set just before the economy in question gets into a recovery, the double-clutch effect will be accompanied with the resonance effect of government investment, the degree of its effectiveness will be strengthened.

4. A Model of Growth Rate Cycles of the Japanese Economy with the Double-Clutch Effect

An attempt to estimate a model of growth rate cycles with the double-clutch effect was made, using quarterly time series data of the postwar Japanese economy. Figure 2 shows the movement of the economic growth rate and that of real government investment since the second quarter of 1958. The economic growth rate shows remarkable cyclical fluctuations during the periods before the first oil crisis, while after the first oil crisis, the economic fluctuations appeared rather complex; that is, the oscillation is not so regular, and its amplitude became smaller than before the first oil crisis.

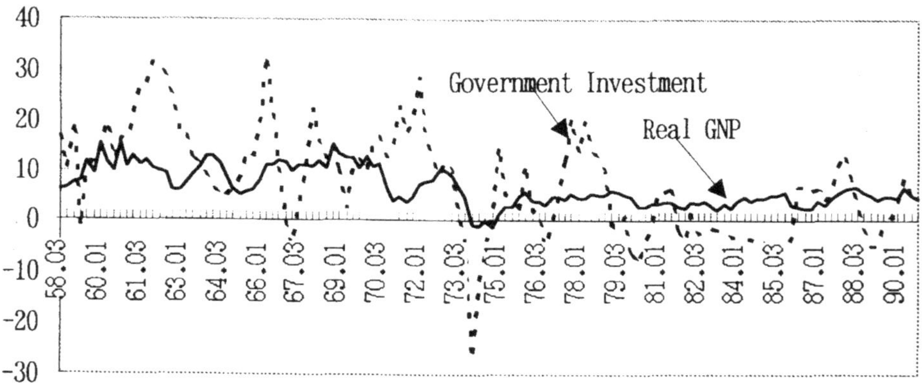

Fig. 2. Growth Rates of Real GNP and Government Investment (Annual rate, %)

Growth rates of real government investment showed fluctuations on a large scale through the observation period, but they showed many negative values after the first oil crisis. It can be easily understood that cyclical aspects of those growth rates clearly changed after the first oil crisis. This suggests that the relationship between economic growth and government investment, as a major factor influencing the former, has also changed after the first oil crisis in Japan.[d]

We will find, using our model in the next sections, that the phase of endogenous oscillation of the economic growth rate coincides with that of government investment in many periods before the first oil crisis, but in few periods after the crisis.

As the non-homogeneous systematic terms of the model, government investment and the official rate of interest of the Bank of Japan were taken into consideration, the time series data on relevant variables showed that the latter policy variable appears to have an asymmetric effect on real economic activity at least in Japan: Although a rise in the official rate has the effect of depressing the economy as a whole, its fall does not necessarily stimulate effective demand. This was confirmed by estimating Eq. (1) with the data split into separate periods of rising and falling official interest rates. Although the estimated coefficient for the rising official rate was found to be significant, that for the falling official rate was not significant during the period from 1958 through 1990.

In order to extract the resonance and the double-clutch effects from the actual fluctuations of the economic growth rate, let us focus our attention on analysis of the effect of government investment to stimulate effective demand, taking account of only the negative effect of a rising official rate. Equation (2) is specified as below:

$$bx^{**}(t) = cx^{*}(t) + e\mathrm{DUM1D} + f\mathrm{DUM1D1}\,, \quad \text{and}$$

$$x^{*}(t) = 0.3x(t+1) + 0.35x(t) + 0.25x(t-1) + 0.1x(t-2)\,, \tag{6}$$

where x is real rate of growth of government investment, DUM1D is a rising value, otherwise zero, of the official rate in the current period, and DUM1D1 is its previous value. The values 0.3, 0.35, 0.25 and 0.1 are weights asigned to the lagged variables. The reason why those arbitrary values were used as weights is to avoid multicollinearity in estimating Eq. (1).

[d]Professor Shishido pointed out that government investment expenditures excludes the investments by the Japan National Railway after its privatization as JR in 1985. We can, however, take this as a decline of public investment, because the investment behavior of JR can be regarded as endogenous after that year. A super multiplier effect of investment of JR should instead be evaluated.

An ordinary least squares estimate of Eq. (1) with the above specification of non-homogeneous terms is:

$$\begin{aligned} y(t) = {} & \underset{(3.16)}{0.990} + \underset{(8.41)}{0.7177}y(t-1) + \underset{(3.69)}{0.3650}y(t-2) - \underset{(1.17)}{0.1235}y(t-3) \\ & - \underset{(4.07)}{0.4023}y(t-4) + \underset{(2.85)}{0.2399}y(t-5) + \underset{(2.07)}{0.0380}x^*(t) \\ & - \underset{(3.13)}{1.7270}\mathrm{DUM1D} + \underset{(3.19)}{1.9381}\mathrm{DUM1D1} \end{aligned} \tag{7}$$

$\mathrm{R}^2 = 0.832 \quad \mathrm{DW} = 1.989 \quad df = 122 \quad (1958{:}1 - 1990{:}3)$

where DUM1D is a dummy variable assuming the values of the actual data of the official rate when it rises, and is otherwise zero. DUM1D1 is its lagged variable. Figures in the parentheses are the corresponding t values, R^2 is the coefficient of determination adjusted for the degree of freedom, DW is the Durbin–Watson ratio, and df is the number of degrees of freedom.

The estimated result shown here is the final one selected after repeating estimation for alternative specifications. Except for the fact that the estimate of the coefficient of the growth rate lagged three quarters is not significant, this estimated result seems to be satisfactory. The estimate of the term for explaining the double-clutch effect of government investment seems to be statistically significant, and its sign is appropriate. The positive sign of the coefficient estimate of the official rate in the previous period can be interpreted to reflect the over-reaction of the economy to the restrictive policy of the monetary authority. It also suggests that the change in the official rate is the appropriate variable for explaining the change in real output.

Using this empirical result, let us obtain the cyclical factors characterizing the endogenous cycles of the Japanese economy. By calculating and solving the homogeneous equation estimated above, one real root and two conjugate complex roots were obtained. Thus, the solution can be written as below:

$$\begin{aligned} y_p(t) &= A_0 0.783^t + A_1(-0.6124 \pm 0.4966i)^t + A_2(0.5818 \pm 0.3910i)^t \\ &= A_0 0.783^t + A_1 0.790^t \cos(129t + \omega_1) + A_2 0.701^t \cos(43t + \omega_2)\,. \end{aligned} \tag{8}$$

According to this solution, the Japanese economy has two cyclical factors. One is the cycle whose period is 8.4 months and whose amplitude dampens to one-half in one-half year. The other is a cycle whose period is 25.1 months and whose amplitude also turns out to be one-half in one-half year. As a whole, the Japanese economy seems to have a stable cyclical structure.[e] Since this solution is for the growth rate, the value of the real root is positive but less than unity.

5. The Resonance and the Double-Clutch Effect of the Japanese Economy

Next, to obtain the cyclical properties of the real growth rate of government investment, a linear difference equation with respect to the real growth rate of government investment was fitted to quarterly time series data during the same observation period that was used for the economic growth rate. The dynamic solution of this estimated equation is to correspond with Eq. (4). By trial and error estimation, the final result was found to be:

$$\begin{aligned} x(t) = {} & \underset{(2.60)}{1.7916} + \underset{(9.48)}{0.7796}x(t-1) + \underset{(1.08)}{0.1120}x(t-2) - \underset{(0.46)}{0.0468}x(t-3) \\ & - \underset{(3.78)}{0.3750}x(t-4) + \underset{(4.34)}{0.3453}x(t-5) - \underset{(4.27)}{8.369}\mathrm{DUM1D} + \underset{(4.08)}{8.847}\mathrm{DUM1D1} \end{aligned} \tag{9}$$

$$R^2 = 0.730 \qquad DW = 2.00 \qquad df = 122 \quad (1958{:}1 - 1990{:}3)\,.$$

Looking at this empirical result, estimates for the coefficients of the real growth rate of government investment at periods $(t-2)$ and $(t-3)$ are not significant, but we use these estimates for the moment.

There may be various interpretations to the fact that government investment has such regular cyclical properties as shown in (9). The reason why the real growth rate of government investment has almost the same cyclical pattern as that of economic growth rate is that changes in aggregate activity guide the direction of changes in government investment. This implies that government investment is induced through changes in its fiscal revenues, so that government investment is not an exogenous policy instrument. Even then, the double-clutch effect of government investment works on the economy as a whole, but this process may or may not take place, depending on whether

[e] At the symposium, Professor Taku Yamamoto of Hitotsubashi University pointed out that the Japanese macro structure is found to be stable in many repeated time-series experiments.

or not the government can manipulate its policy instruments appropriately, faced with economic fluctuations.

If government investment is determined by its own discretionary policy, it is quite difficult to understand this phenomenon. In this case, an independent decision of the government to change its investment is made cyclically. It should be understood that because of a strong tendency for the level of real output to influence the size of government budget, such a cyclical property of government investment is observed. Even if this is the case, the oscillatory pattern of government investment surely has a large impact on the macroeconomy through the multiplier process.

In particular, if in addition to the fact that the periods of oscillation of the macroeconomy and government investment almost coincide with each other, their phases are also equal to each other, the amplitude of the fluctuation of the macroeconomy is enlarged, and the use of fiscal policy as an anti-cyclical policy may excessively drive the macroeconomy into an unstable situation. At this point, the cyclical property of government investment poses a serious problem in keeping the macroeconomy on a steady growth path. It is also conceivable that even if the nominal value of government investment is effectively determined by government, its real growth rate may have a cyclical property that is synchronized with the macroeconomy, through market price adjustments that reflect demand for and supply of goods and services. Further plausible explanation of the relationship is needed.

The solution for the homogeneous part of (9) can be written as below:

$$\begin{aligned} x_p(t) &= B_0 0.875^t + B_1(-0.5909 \pm 0.5436i)^t + B_2(0.5436 \pm 0.5625i)^t \\ &= B_0 0.875^t + B_1 0.803^t \cos(133t + \sigma_1) + B_2 0.782^t \cos(46t + \sigma_2)\,. \quad (10) \end{aligned}$$

This empirical result shows that one oscillatory period is 8.1 months, and the oscillation dampens to one-half in one-half year. The other period is 23.5 months, and the oscillation also damps to half in half a year. Here, to be stressed is that the cyclical properties closely resemble those of the economic growth rate and the real rate of growth of government investment. This implies that there is a strong possibility that the business cycle generates resonance phenomena caused by a change in government investment.

Many economists, including myself, have observed that the amplitude of business cycles has recently been decreasing. The question is, what causes this? Here, we will examine the tracks of the double-clutch effect of government investment, and also examine how the business cycles have reacted to recent changes in government investment.

As already discussed, the possibility of generating resonance phenomena seems to be high during the observation period. It is necessary to examine whether or not the phase of endogenous cycles of the economic growth rate coincides with that of the real growth rate of government investment for the observation period since 1958. To do this, we first obtain the complete form of the dynamic solution of Eq. (1); second, we compare its phase with that of the solution for the real growth rate of government investment, obtained from Eqs. (2) and (4), and third, we examine whether there is any significant oscillation in the period during which the coincidence of the two phases is observed. In order for the double-clutch effect to work, the phase of endogenous cycles of economic growth should lead the phase of the real growth rate of government investment by one quarter.

As is well known, the value of the phase depends on the initial values of all variables included in the difference equation in question, so that the value of the phase should be calculated for each period. As the initial values for the solutions (8) and (10), the observed values for each quarterly period from the second quarter of 1958 through the third quarter of 1990 were used.

Table 1 shows the results of calculation of values of the phase for each solution with the initial values. In this table, only the three cases where both pairs of phases were almost equal to each other are listed.

It is seen, in the table, that these phases are similar to each other. In particular, ω_1 and σ_1; and ω_2 and σ_2 are fairly close to each other, respectively. It seems clear that these three periods correspond with those periods in which economic growth rate cycles actually appear, by referring to Fig. 2. In each case, growth rate cycles appeared two quarters after the corresponding phase of government investment. The reason why this lag is observed is not clear.

Table 1. Comparison of the Phases for Economic Growth and Government Investment Period.

Period	ω_1	ω_2	σ_1	σ_2
1962:2	49.4	55.8	46.8	57.0
1971:1	50.0	66.3	46.1	65.1
1988:1	52.1	55.7	46.2	68.1

The endogenous economic growth rate cycles and real growth rate cycles of government investment have, as already observed, a short period of about 8 months and a long period of about 25 months; that is, they oscillate over a longer cycle with a period of about 25 months, repeating a small cycle with a period of about 8 months. It may be more realistic to compare the phases with the longer cycles. The results of a comparison of the similarity of phases between the economic growth rate and the real growth rate of government investment are in Table 2.

It is clear that those periods correspond well with the periods at which economic growth rate cycles appear. The first 4 periods are the "Iwato" boom starting in June, 1958; the next 2 periods are the "Izanagi" boom starting in October, 1965. The next 3 periods and the last period also correspond with booms. It should again be emphasized that in those periods, the double-clutch effect of government investment certainly worked so as to generate big booms. The interesting thing is that there is no period in which the phases of both cycles are similar to each other in the 1980s. But, this does not mean that the double-clutch effect of government investment has already disappeared. To analyze this in more detail, the structural change in the macroeconomy after the first oil crisis should be taken into account.

Table 2. Comparison of the Phases for Economic Growth and Government Investment: The Longer Cycles.

Period	ω_2	σ_2
1959:1	54.1	50.6
1959:3	46.6	48.1
1960:2	58.4	56.7
1962:2	55.8	57.0
1966:1	52.5	53.0
1970:2	57.3	59.4
1971:1	66.3	65.1
1971:4	57.3	58.8
1972:1	51.7	49.5
1977:3	62.8	63.0

6. Economic Growth Rate Cycles after the First Oil Crisis

In order to clearify when structural change in the Japanese economy has taken place, the "Chow Test" or other statistical tests of structural change could be used. The purpose of this study, however, is not to search the period for evidence of change, but to examine whether or not the double-clutch effect of government investment still exists after the structural change of our economy has taken place. Taking account of time lags included in our equation, we choose the observation periods after the fourth quarter of 1976; so Eq. (1) was reestimated for the period from the first quarter of 1977 through the fourth quarter of 1991. The estimated result is:

$$\begin{aligned} y(t) = {} & \underset{(3.06)}{2.604} + \underset{(6.91)}{0.6894}y(t-1) - \underset{(1.72)}{0.2197}y(t-4) + \underset{(1.95)}{0.2670}y(t-5) - \underset{(2.12)}{0.2460}y(t-6) \\ & + \underset{(1.20)}{0.0222}x^*(t) - \underset{(0.98)}{0.0751}r_m - \underset{(3.22)}{1.972}\mathrm{DUM1D} + \underset{(3.35)}{4.324}\mathrm{DUM1D1} \end{aligned} \tag{11}$$

$R^2 = 0.583 \qquad DW = 2.15 \qquad df = 51$

where r_m is the average market yield of the NTT bond. The estimated result seems to be considerably different from that for the whole period. This indicates that a structural change has taken place after the first oil crisis in the Japanese economy. The reason for adding the NTT rate as an explanatory variable in the non-homogeneous term is to take account of a growing influence of financial markets on real economic activities. The estimate for the coefficient, however, was not significant. It cannot be said that the estimate of the coefficient of x^* is significantly different from zero, and this implies that the double-clutch effect does not work, on the average in a statistical sense, after the first oil crisis. To make sure of this, it is necessary to examine whether or not there is any period in which the phases of economic growth rate cycles and the cycles of the real rate of growth of government investment coincide with each other.

The solution for the homogeneous equation of (8) can be written as below:

$$\begin{aligned} y_p(t) = {} & (-18.1)0.847^t \cos(25.5t + 30.3) + (110.8)0.713^t \cos(80.9t + 61.8) \\ & + (43.7)0.821^t \cos(157.6t - 64.3), \end{aligned} \tag{12}$$

where the values based on the initial condition are used, which are averaged, because they did not show any systematic change for changes in the initial condition. The oscillatory periods calculated from the solution above were 42, 13 and 7 months respectively.

Next, an equation for real growth rate of government investment was also estimated for the same observation period as (11). The best result was:

$$\begin{aligned} x(t) = {} & \underset{(1.80)}{1.074} + \underset{(6.34)}{0.8558}x(t-1) + \underset{(0.45)}{0.0805}x(t-2) - \underset{(0.74)}{0.1272}x(t-3) - \underset{(2.27)}{0.3711}x(t-4) \\ & + \underset{(2.73)}{0.3788}x(t-5) - \underset{(1.03)}{3.454}\mathrm{DUM1D} + \underset{(0.86)}{3.393}\mathrm{DUM1D1}\,. \end{aligned} \tag{13}$$

$R^2 = 0.694 \qquad DW = 1.75 \qquad df = 47$

This result is not entirely satisfactory, but for the moment, I will use it to examine whether or not the double-clutch effect still works in certain periods. The solution of the equation above is as follows:

$$\begin{aligned} x_p(t) = {} & (-17.838)0.8744^t - (97.0)0.7960^t \cos(41.9t + 64.7) \\ & + (31.5)0.8268^t \cos(45.2t - 6.2)\,. \end{aligned} \tag{14}$$

The oscillatory periods obtained from the solution above were 26 months and 24 months. As can be easily seen, the period of economic growth rate cycles appears quite different from that of the real growth rate of government investment. Moreover, despite the fact that the phase of endogenous economic growth rate cycles is 64.7 degrees, that of government investment is 30.3 degrees, by offsetting the other two phases, 61.8 and −64.3; therefore, economic growth rate cycles and the cycles of the real growth rate of government investment hardly generate resonance phenomena.

7. Concluding Remarks

In this study, it was attempted to clarify the characteristics of economic growth rate cycles of Japan since the 1950s, by asserting that when a macroeconomic policy designed to stimulate effective demand turns out to be a problem, government should be more conscious of its timing of execution by relying on the resonance/double-clutch effect of government investment. Based on the resonance effect considered theoretically by Allen and Hicks, and tested empirically by Kei Mori, the author developed the double-clutch effect of government investment, and found that during periods of high economic growth in Japan, the resonance/double-clutch effect of government investment certainly worked, but after the first oil crisis, this effect was found not to work clearly.

This, however, does not imply that there is no possibility for this effect to work. For instance, a large scale increase in government expenditures has recently been planned by the government to stimulate domestic demand more rigorously in order to accelerate the recovery from the recession that prevails now. If the recovery as a result of endogenous cycles of economic growth rate has already begun, then now is the time to add a stimulus to the domestic market.

Finally, it should be noticed that the double-clutch effect has different implications for the expectations of the public as compared with the so-called "rational expectations". The preparatory stage of government investment may change the expectations of the public, and the rational behavior of the public will be revised, but it does not follow that the effect of government policy will be neutralized. At the same time, it should also be emphasized that the public will form expections about the multiplier effect of government investment in advance.

Acknowledgments

The author is grateful to Professor Lawrence R. Klein, Professor Shuntaro Shishido and other participants at the Conference for their useful comments. The idea for this study stemmed from [Kei Mori, 1967/1993]. I sent to him a final long comment on his work which was late. A topic which I discussed with a student who belonged to the Automobile Club of Keio University, Hisatake Chikaraishi inspired me to develop this study.

Comments and suggestions of S. Nakamura and M. Hikari of Keio University were very helpful. Discussions with M. Nishino of Meiji University at the Meeting of the Japan Association of Economic Policies, May, 1992, and with Dr. H. Motamen-Scobie and others at the International Symposium on Economic Modeling, Athens, June, 1993 were also useful.

References

1. R. G. D. Allen, *Mathematical Economics* (Macmillan, London, 1956), p. 227.
2. R. M. Goodwin, "The non-linear accelerator and the persistence of business cycles," *Econometrica*, vol. **19**, pp. 1–17 (1951).
3. F. Hamada, "A macroeconomic model with the rate of unemployment as a risk probability under the government budget restraint," in eds. K. Uno and

S. Shishido, *Statistical Data Bank Systems: Socio-Economic Database and Model Building in Japan* (North-Holland, Amsterdam, 1988), pp. 65–79.

4. J. R. Hicks, *A Contribution to the Theory of the Trade Cycle* (Clarendon Press, Oxford, 150), p. 201.
5. K. Mori, *A Macroeconometric Simulation Analysis of the Postwar Japanese Economy, 1953–1961* (Yuhikaku Publishing Co., 1967/1993).

COMMENTS ON FUMIMASA HAMADA'S "A MODEL OF GROWTH RATE CYCLES AND THE RESONANCE/DOUBLE-CLUTCH EFFECT OF PUBLIC INVESTMENT"

SHUNTARO SHISHIDO

This paper is very interesting, as it deals with a combined effect on the GNP growth rate, an announcement effect and an execution of public investment in the context of a Keynesian macroeconomic growth rate model of Japan, on a quarterly basis since the first quarter of 1958. The model is an extension of Kei Mori's version of "a resonance effect" of Japan's monetary policy, theoretically developed by [Allen, 1956] and [Hicks, 1950]. The paper has an important policy implication at the present time, when the Japanese economy is still weakly recovering from its worst post-war recession.

In Hamada's paper, the quarterly growth rate of real GNP is accounted for by its auto-regressive parameters and the changes in government investment and interest rate as exogenous variables. By deriving particular solutions from his sinusoidal functions he successfully obtained interesting parameters for Japan's cyclical properties of GNP movement and government investment, i.e., parameters for the cycle period, phase, and timing. His findings are particularly important as it covers a long period between 1958 and 1990, including both the pre- and the post-oil price shock periods.

My first comment is related to his OLS estimate of Eq. (1) for the entire period from 1958 through 1990. As can be seen from Fig. 2, there is a sharp drop in the GNP growth rate after the first oil price shock, attributable in part to a similar decline in the growth rate of government investment. As compared with another OLS estimate of the GNP growth rate after the oil price shock for 1977 through 1991, there seems to be a significant structural shift in terms of GNP growth rate response. Since his paper places more emphasis upon the existence of a "double-clutch effect," the paper describes very little about a structural issue. However, the explicit treatment of this issue in my opinion, could have enhanced the strength of his empirical findings. As pointed out by many analysts, there is a dramatic change in policy stance of the Japanese government since the first oil price shock in 1974. Business and bureaucrats, especially the MITI, overreacted in terms of energy supply constraints, thus leading to a weaker policy stance toward economic growth. In terms of power politics, the influence of the Ministry of Finance, always the strongest proponent of the balanced budget principle, became relatively stronger, supported by another group of neo-liberalists arguing for a smaller government and budget. The group centered around proponents for RINCHO — Special Government Committee for Administrative Reform. In my view, such a political shift factor after the late 1970s and during the 1980s needs to be explicitly taken into account in Hamada's OLS estimation for the entire period.

My second comment on his OLS estimation is related to the data on government investment. As is widely known, JR (Japan Railway Company) and NTT (Nippon Telephone and Telecommunication Company) were privatized in the first quarter of 1985 and 1987, respectively. This represents a dramatic decline in government investment in these sectors, as shown in Fig. 2. This decline should be treated by the use of dummy variables, thus improving estimates for both the entire period and the latter half, after the first oil shock.

THE ROLE OF CHARACTERISTIC ROOTS IN DYNAMIC ECONOMIC SYSTEMS

LAWRENCE R. KLEIN
Benjamin Franklin Professor of Economics
Emeritus
University of Pennsylvania

1. Introduction

The properties of mathematical models of the economy can be studied in terms of the values of parameters of the systems involved. The characteristic roots (eigenvalues) of systems are combinations or functions of the parameters, and they summarize a great deal of information about system properties — information that might otherwise remain obscure. The analysis of roots provides an informative way of learning about system properties.

I have chosen this subject of investigation in the present paper because Kei Mori, the central figure of this symposium, arrived in Philadelphia in 1968, full of fresh ideas about the evaluation of characteristic roots of linear dynamic systems. The concept of characteristic roots is not so complicated, but, as will be shown in this essay, they are very involved functions of system parameters, and the numerical evaluation of roots, or properties of roots, is not so simple. Also there was need, especially in the computer environment of 1968, to be very careful about root evaluation, and to simplify the procedures as much as possible.

In small models, root evaluation can be very straightforward and simple, but roots had not been estimated — except by Jan Tinbergen — in large systems involving hundreds or more parameters; and we were involved, at Pennsylvania, in computing the roots of a simplified version of the then prevailing Wharton Model, just at the time that Kei Mori appeared on the scene.

Tinbergen reduced, through approximation, his moderately large system to a difference equation of low order.

A linearized, small version of the Wharton Model had just been prepared, and E. P. Howrey was using a particular algorithm to compute the roots; Kei Mori was using a different one that he had constructed. Most of the estimated roots agreed between the two approaches, but there were some particular roots that Howrey had found (real roots 0.962 and 0.865) and some different ones (complex roots 0.819 ± 0.193i and 0.825 ± 0.088i) that Kei Mori had found. The absolute values of the two complex roots are approximately 0.84 and 0.83 respectively — comparable to one of the two real roots that Howrey found but not as large as 0.962.

Computational hardware and software are much more accurate today, but large systems presented analytical challenges during the 1960s. It is instructive to look at the whole question of characteristic roots to see how they are related to a system's structure and what insights they provide into a system's properties or performance.

Roots of Linear Dynamic Systems, Simple Examples

Let us take the simplest possible system, a first order autoregressive process, in which a variable is a function of its preceding value

$$y_t = \alpha y_{t-1} \,. \tag{1}$$

It is easy, and instructive, to work out the solution to this equation, step-by-step, just the way it would be solved arithmetically (digitally) on a computer. Start with an initial value, y_0, then the next value is

$$y_1 = \alpha y_0 \,,$$

and the next value, after that, is

$$y_2 = \alpha y_1 = \alpha(\alpha y_0) = \alpha^2 y_0 \,.$$

The general solution is immediately recognizable as

$$y_t = \alpha^t y_0 \,.$$

It turns out, in this simplest of all cases, that α is the only characteristic root of this single-equation, first-order (lag) system. In (1), α is a parameter (or coefficient), and the characteristic root happens to be such a simple function of α that it is, in fact, α.

If

$$-1 < \alpha < +1$$

or

$$|\alpha| < 1$$

then $y_t \to 0$ because $\alpha^t \to 0$ as $t \to \infty$. The steady-state or long run solution is $y = 0$.

If this system is generalized so that y_t is expressed as a deviation from its long run value; i.e.,

$$y_t = Y_t - \hat{Y}$$

the basic equation becomes

$$Y_t - \hat{Y} = \alpha(Y_{t-1} - \hat{Y}) \tag{1)'$$

and the general solution is

$$(Y_t - \hat{Y}) = \alpha^t(Y_0 - \hat{Y})$$

As $t \to \infty$, if $|\alpha| < 1$, we have

$$(Y_t - \hat{Y}) \to 0 \text{ or } Y_t \to \hat{Y}.$$

If

$$\alpha > 1$$

y_t grows geometrically, and if

$$\alpha < -1$$

y_t oscillates explosively in a saw-tooth pattern. If $\alpha = -1$, the saw-tooth is a maintained oscillation of constant amplitude, while if $\alpha = +1$, y_t does not change; it always equals its previous value.

In this case, the characteristic root tells us all we want to know about this system's dynamic characteristics, but α, the parameter of the system, tells us that, as well.

Does Eq. (1) have any significance for economics? The answer is, yes. There are at least two interesting cases that lead to first-order systems; one is from growth theory, and the other is from a market clearing version of the "law of supply and demand."

A version of Harrod–Domar growth theory can be expressed, in the simplest case, as

$$\begin{aligned} S_t &= \alpha Y_t;\ K_t = \beta Y_t;\ S_t = K_t - K_{t-1} \\ S_t &= \text{savings (national)} \\ Y_t &= \text{output (national)} \\ K_t &= \text{stock of capital (national)}\,. \end{aligned} \tag{2}$$

In this model, α is a structural parameter, known as the propensity to save (both average and marginal); β is the capital–output ratio

By substitution, this system can be written as

$$S_t = \alpha Y_t$$

$$K_t - K_{t-1} = \beta(Y_t - Y_{t-1}) = S_t$$

or

$$\alpha Y_t = \beta(Y_t - Y_{t-1})$$

This can be reduced to

$$(\beta - \alpha)Y_t = \beta Y_{t-1}$$

or

$$Y_t = \frac{\beta}{\beta - \alpha} Y_{t-1} \tag{3}$$

This equation shows how a small system with a savings relation and a capital–output relation can be reduced to a first-order autoregressive system like (1). The autoregressive coefficient has meaning as a function of two economic parameters, α and β.

This (final) autoregressive equation has a solution

$$Y_t = \left(\frac{\beta}{\beta - \alpha}\right)^t Y_0 .$$

In terms of current data for the United States, the capital–output ratio, β, is roughly 2.0, while the ratio of GDP minus consumer and public spending to GDP is roughly 10 percent. We could put α at 0.10. For this pair of values

$$\frac{\beta}{\beta - \alpha} = \frac{2.0}{1.9} \sim 1.05$$

$$Y_t = (1.05)^t Y_0 .$$

It is not too bad to say that nominal GDP is growing at about 5% annually. For the roughly estimated values of β and α, the characteristic root of the system indicates the long-term growth rate. We can thus interpret the root as a realistic historical property of the system and as a function of structural parameters, β and α.

This system can readily be generalized to allow for openness of the macroeconomy, i.e., to allow for exporting and importing (trading with other countries). This produces the "two-gap" model used for studying growth and development in open economies.[a]

Let us now consider the classic Cobweb model of supply and demand

$$\begin{aligned} S_t &= \alpha_0 + \alpha_1 P_{t-1} \\ D_t &= \beta_0 + \beta_1 P_t \\ S_t &= D_t . \end{aligned} \tag{4}$$

In this simple model, supply is said to depend on previous price, demand on present price; and supply and demand are equated to clear the market. A perishable crop, with t designating crop seasons, gives rise to this kind of model.

[a]The two-gap model, due to Hollis Chenery, has been estimated to study Chinese economic growth, Youcai Liang and Lawrence R. Klein, "The two-gap paradigm in the Chinese case: A pedagogical exercise," *China Economic Review*, I (Spring 1989), 1–8.

The model can, by substitution, be reduced to

$$\beta_0 + \beta_1 P_t = \alpha_0 + \alpha_1 P_{t-1}$$

$$P_t = \frac{\alpha_0 - \beta_0}{\beta_1} + \frac{\alpha_1}{\beta_1} P_{t-1} \,.$$

Apart from the introduction of a constant term, this equation has the same mathematical form as (1). It is a first-order autoregression between P_t and P_{t-1}. The introduction of the constant term makes it like (1)′.

The characteristic root of (4) is α_1/β_1, the ratio of the price response in supply to that in demand. In logarithmic quantities, it would be the ratio of the price elasticity of supply to the price elasticity of demand.

If

$$\alpha_1 > 0 \,, \quad \beta_1 < 0 \,,$$

the usual case, we find a (saw-tooth) oscillation of price. It will be a damped saw-tooth fluctuation if

$$|\alpha_1| < |\beta_1|$$

and an explosive one if

$$|\alpha_1| > |\beta_1| \,.$$

In the unusual case

$$|\alpha_1| = |\beta_1|$$

it will be a perfectly maintained saw-tooth oscillation that does not die down or expand in amplitude.

Just as the Harrod–Domar model has been extended to allow for international trade and price determination, so has the cobweb model been generalized to allow for longer time delays on the supply side and incomplete market clearing through the introduction of inventory holdings, and, in the case of manufactured products, the simultaneous production of scrap. Generalizations like these leave the core analysis intact, with add-on elaboration, and extensions of dynamic analysis through study of characteristic roots.

At this stage, it is useful to move to the next order of difficulty, by allowing for a second-order autoregressive process, which produces two characteristic roots and thereby introduces entirely new considerations.

A slight generalization of the Harrod–Domar model is

$$
\begin{aligned}
C_t &= \alpha Y_{t-1} \\
I_t &= \beta(Y_{t-1} - Y_{t-2}) \\
Y_t &= C_t + I_t \\
C_t &= \text{consumer spending (national)} \\
Y_t &= \text{output (national)} \\
I_t &= \text{investment (national)}\,.
\end{aligned}
\tag{5}
$$

Instead of writing the (closed) system explicitly in terms of saving and investment, it is written in terms of consumer spending and investment. Saving behavior is implied by substituting

$$S_t = Y_t - C_t$$

into (5). We then get

$$
\begin{aligned}
S_t &= Y_t - C_t = Y_t - \alpha Y_{t-1} \\
S_t &= I_t = \beta(Y_{t-1} - Y_{t-2})\,.
\end{aligned}
$$

The final autoregressive equation is

$$
\begin{aligned}
Y_t - \alpha Y_{t-1} &= \beta(Y_{t-1} - Y_{t-2}) \\
Y_t - (\alpha + \beta)Y_{t-1} + \beta Y_{t-2} &= 0\,.
\end{aligned}
$$

A way of solving this second-order equation is to try

$$y_t = K\lambda^t$$

as a solution. K, in this context, stands for an arbitrary constant. By substitution into the second-order lag equation for Y_t, we get

$$K\lambda^t - (\alpha + \beta)K\lambda^{t-1} + \beta K\lambda^{t-2} = 0$$

$$\lambda^2 - (\alpha + \beta)\lambda + \beta = 0\,. \tag{6}$$

Equation (6) is the characteristic equation for this second-order system, and the solution, by application of the quadratic formula, is

$$\lambda = \frac{(\alpha+\beta) \pm \sqrt{(\alpha+\beta)^2 - 4\beta}}{2} .$$

Now we have an entirely new kind of expression for the characteristic roots. There can be as many as two roots, and they can be either real or imaginary. Also, the relation between λ, the characteristic root, and the coefficients is not as simple as in the previous example. There is, nevertheless, a specific relation between λ, on the one hand, and α, β, on the other.

This model, which may be called the multiplier–accelerator model, has been analyzed by Edwin Kuh, John Neese, and Peter Hollinger, in some detail.[b] They consider, for example, $\alpha = 0.75$ and $\beta = 0.25$. In that case, both roots are equal

$$\begin{aligned}\lambda &= \frac{(0.75+0.25) \pm \sqrt{(0.75+0.25)^2 - 4(0.25)}}{2} \\ &= \frac{1 \pm \sqrt{1-1}}{2} = 1/2\end{aligned}$$

and the model has, in this sense, a structural defect. Not only are these roots very special, they are unlikely in an economic context because β is essentially a capital–output ratio — in first difference form, i.e., an "i-corr" ratio. It would hardly be as small as 0.25.

For $\beta = 2$ and $\alpha = 0.6$, much more likely values — not out of line with data for the US economy – we find conjugate complex roots. The system oscillates in a sinusoidal pattern, but also diverges.

$$\begin{aligned}\lambda &= \frac{(2.6) \pm \sqrt{(2.6)^2 - 8}}{2} \\ &= \frac{2.6 \pm \sqrt{-1.24}}{2} .\end{aligned}$$

[b]Edwin Kuh, John W. Neese, and Peter Hollinger, *Structural Sensitivity in Econometric Models* (John Wiley & Sons, New York, 1985) pp. 72 ff.

Since λ is conjugate complex in this case, the absolute value is

$$|\lambda| = \sqrt{\frac{6.76}{4} + \frac{1.24}{4}}$$
$$= \sqrt{2} > 1\,.$$

These are not the best parameter values, but they are plausible, and the analysis of the roots indicates that they are not generally acceptable since we do not generally observe this kind of explosive behavior. The problem is not necessarily one of this particular model; it is more a case of expanding the system to allow explicitly for *openness*, a stabilizing tax-transfer system, and a role for key exogenous variables, as with monetary policy.

As we moved from the Harrod–Domar model, with one real root, to Samuelson's multiplier–accelerator model, we found a richer range of possibilities, with two roots. They could, however, be degenerate, or both real, or both complex. For example with $\alpha = 0.9$ instead of 0.6 and $\beta = 2$, the roots are both real (and greater than 1.0). Slight changes in the model or in parameter values can make significant differences in the root-structure and change the nature of the system's performance greatly. The calculation of the roots tells us a great deal about the system and its sensitivity to specification.

Still within the realm of simple models let us consider an interesting example from market analysis, as distinct from the macroeconomics of growth or business cycle analysis. A model due to Francis Dresch is

$$D_t = \alpha_0 + \alpha_1 P_t \quad \text{demand function}$$
$$S_t = \beta_0 + \beta_1 P_t \quad \text{supply function}$$
$$\Delta P_t = -\lambda \sum_{i=-\infty}^{t-1} (S_i - D_i)\,. \tag{7}$$

By substitution, this reduces to

$$\Delta^2 P_t = P_t - 2P_{t-1} + P_{t-2}$$
$$= -\lambda(\beta_1 - \alpha_1)P_{t-1} - \lambda(\beta_0 - \alpha_0)$$
$$P_t - (2 - \lambda')P_{t-1} + P_{t-2} = -\lambda(\beta_0 - \alpha_0) \tag{8}$$

where

$$\lambda' = \lambda(\beta_1 - \alpha_1)\,.$$

The characteristic equation for this second-order system is

$$\mu^2 - (2 - \lambda')\mu + 1 = 0$$

with roots

$$\mu = \frac{2 - \lambda' \pm \sqrt{(2 - \lambda')^2 - 4}}{2}\,.$$

If

$$(2 - \lambda')^2 < 4$$

the solution has a conjugate complex pair of roots with modulus 1.0

$$|\mu| = \frac{(2 - \lambda')^2 - (2 - \lambda')^2 + 4}{4} = 1\,.$$

This part of the solution generates an undamped sinusoidal fluctuation. The characteristic equation is essentially an autoregression of $P_t + P_{t-2}$ on P_{t-1}, with slope coefficient $(2 - \lambda')$, which is less than 1.0 because it is an average of two first-order serial correlations, P_t with P_{t-1} and P_{t-2} with P_{t-1}. The condition that the roots be conjugate complex will be satisfied.

This is a very neat explanation of inventory fluctuations and obviously motivated Francis Dresch's introduction of this process. It has, however, been pointed out by Paul Samuelson that an undamped dynamic movement will generate increasing *variance* over time if an additive error is introduced.[c] This brings us to stochastic considerations and dampening factors will have to be used in order that the stochastic version of this dynamic process makes sense. If the variance of fluctuation grows over time, a confidence interval for prediction will grow without bounds; therefore a form of instability that is not observed in practice will result.

The preceding analysis shows that we must consider the stochastic implications of the systems that are being specified. There is yet another consideration.

[c]P. A. Samuelson, *Foundations of Economic Analysis* (Harvard University Press, Cambridge, 1947).

To see the implications of both stochastic terms and exogenous variables, we can most readily generalize Eq. (1).

$$
\begin{aligned}
y_t &= \alpha y_{t-1} + \beta x_t + e_t \\
x_t &= \text{exogenous variable} \\
e_t &= \text{random error} \\
y_1 &= \alpha y_0 + \beta x_1 + e_1 \\
y_2 &= \alpha y_1 + \beta x_2 + e_2 = \alpha^2 y_0 + \alpha\beta x_1 + \beta x_2 + \alpha e_1 + e_2 \\
&\vdots \\
y_t &= \alpha^t y_0 + \beta \sum_{i=0}^{t-1} \alpha^i x_{t-i} + \sum_{i=0}^{t-1} a^i e_{t-i}\,.
\end{aligned}
\tag{1)''
$$

There are three terms on the rhs, and each needs separate explanation.

(i) $\alpha^t y_0$.

In this expression α is the characteristic root of the first-order process, as well as the autoregressive coefficient. If the root is less than unity

$$|\alpha| < 1\,,$$

the influence of this term eventually fades away. If it is positive and greater than unity, it shows the inherent growth rate of the process, as in the Harrod–Domar growth model.

y_0 is the initial condition of the process; its influence fades as $t \to \infty$ if $|\alpha| < 1$.

(ii) $\beta \sum_{i=0}^{t-1} \alpha^i x_{t-i}$

This is a new part of the solution. It is a moving weighted sum of the exogenous influences. It depends on the time path of x_t and on the weights, α^i. If $|\alpha| < 1$, the weights become smaller, the more distant in time is the i super/subscript. The reverse is true if $|\alpha| > 1$.

(iii) $\sum_{i=0}^{t-1} \alpha^i e_{t-i}$

In stochastic economics, which is important for econometrics, we cannot neglect the influence of errors, both past and present. Historical errors get weighted just as exogenous variables do by powers of the autoregressive coefficient (or the characteristic root). As we shall see in the next section, weighted moving sums of random errors can have very interesting properties.

If

$$|\alpha| \geq 1$$

the variance of the solution for y_t in a dynamic stochastic process grows over time. This was noted by Samuelson (see note 3, above) for the Dresch model of price fluctuations in a simple, second-order inventory process, but it was independently noted by Kalecki, in connection with the stochastic process generating the lognormal distribution.[d] Treatment of the general case for linear simultaneous equations is provided by Mann and Wald.[e]

Finally, we shall close this introductory section with an analysis of the characteristics of a third-order system, that has been used a great deal as a pedagogical example. It admits both real and conjugate complex roots and is about as simple as a system can be in describing the role of characteristic roots, beyond the obvious cases of first- and second-order systems described above.

The system to be considered consists of six equations; three are stochastic and three are accounting identities. The system is known as Klein's Model I. It was developed in the late 1940s and published in 1950. It has been used as an example for various econometric exercises.

$$\begin{aligned} C_t &= \alpha_0 + \alpha_1 \Pi_t + \alpha_2 \Pi_{t-1} + \alpha_3 (W_{1t} + W_{2t}) + e_{1t} \\ I_t &= \beta_0 + \beta_1 \Pi_t + \beta_2 \Pi_{t-1} + \beta_3 K_{t-1} + e_{2t} \\ W_{1t} &= \gamma_0 + \gamma_1 (Y_t + T_t - W_{2t}) + \gamma_2 (Y_{t-1} + T_{t-1} - W_{2t-1}) \\ &\quad + \gamma_3 (t - 1931) + e_{3t} \end{aligned} \tag{9}$$

[d] M. Kalecki, "On the Gibrat distribution," *Econometrica* **13**, 161–70 (1945).

[e] H. B. Mann and A. Wald, "On the statistical treatment of linear stochastic difference equations," *Econometrica*, **11** 173–220 (July–October, 1943).

$$Y_t + T_t = C_t + I_t + G_t$$

$$Y_t = \Pi_t + W_{1t} + W_{2t}$$

$$K_t - K_{t-1} = I_t \, .$$

This system has been estimated by various methods. Using the variant by limited-information–maximum-likelihood, we get

$$\begin{aligned} &\alpha_0 = 17.71\,, \quad \alpha_1 = 0.02\,, \quad \alpha_2 = 0\,, \quad \alpha_3 = 0.87 \\ &\beta_0 = 22.59\,, \quad \beta_1 = 0.08\,, \quad \beta_2 = 0.68\,, \quad \beta_3 = -0.17 \\ &\gamma_0 = 1.53\,, \quad \gamma_1 = 0.43\,, \quad \gamma_2 = 0.15\,, \quad \gamma_3 = 0.13\,. \end{aligned}$$

This numerical system reduces to the final autoregressive form

$$\begin{aligned} 0.57Y_t = {} & 0.97Y_{t-1} - 0.58Y_{t-2} + 0.10Y_{t-3} + 3.22 \\ & + 0.02(t - 1931) + 0.44(W_2)_t - 0.18(W_2)_{t-1} - 0.10(W_2)_{t-2} \\ & - 0.10(W_2)_{t-3} - 0.67T_t + 0.38T_{t-1} + 0.10T_{t-2} + 0.10T_{t-3} \\ & + G - 0.83G_{t-1} + e_{1t} - 0.83(e_1)_{t-1} + e_{2t} - (e_2)_{t-1} + 0.77e_{3t} \\ & - 1.31(e_3)_{t-1} + 0.68(e_3)_{t-2}\,. \end{aligned} \tag{10}$$

The characteristic equation is

$$0.57Y_t - 0.97Y_{t-1} + 0.58Y_{t-2} - 0.10Y_{t-3} = 0\,,$$

and the roots are

$$0.292\,;\ 0.704 + 0.344i\,;\ 0.704 - 0.344i\,.$$

The absolute value of the complex pair is 0.78; so the fluctuation is stable, with a 14-year period.

Theil and Boot used the estimates of the same model obtained by the method of full-information–maximum-likelihood and found roots.[f]

$$0.334\,;\ 0.838\,(\cos 0.435 + i \sin 0.435) = 0.759 + 0.352i\,;$$

$$0.838\,(\cos 0.435 - i \sin 0.435) = 0.759 - 0.352i$$

[f] H. Theil and J. C. G. Boot, "The final form of econometric equation systems," *Review of the International Statistical Institute*, **30**, 136–52 (1962).

In this section, I have examined simple cases in which the characteristic roots are readily obtained and also expressed in closed-form from the solution of low order characteristic (polynomials) equations. These lend themselves to economic interpretation in terms of well-known trends and cycles.

It is to be noted that the final autoregressive form contained linear combinations of lagged values of exogenous variables and error terms. These are dropped in the linear case for the analysis of dynamic properties of the trends and cycles. That part of the analysis is interesting, but misses some crucial points that are important for the analysis of the full contribution of the roots to the solution.

The complete solution to the supply-demand model with price adjustment to inventory stock can be obtained from the stochastic form of the characteristic equation.[g]

$$P_t - (2 - \lambda')P_{t-1} + P_{t-2} = -\lambda(\beta_0 - \alpha_0) + e_t - e_{t-1} \tag{8'}$$

as

$$P_t = C_1\mu_1^t + C_2\mu_2^t + \sum_{i=0}^{t-2} \frac{\mu_1^{j+1} - \mu_2^{j+1}}{\mu_1 - \mu_2}\left[e_{t-j} - e_{t-1-j} - \lambda(\beta_0 - \alpha_0)\right]. \tag{11}$$

The roots μ_1 and μ_2 are distinct. They influence both parts of the solution — the general solution of the homogeneous function and the particular solution. In the next section, I shall have more to say about the interpretation of the particular solution involving the random error terms.

The General Linear Dynamic Model

In the previous section, I tried to show how characteristic roots appear in the solutions of some simple models, all of which can be interpreted in terms of well-known economic examples. The general linear model can, however, be of large dimension. Dynamic models of the macroeconomy and of specific sectors often have more than 100 equations, with several finite lags. In many cases, the number of equations may even run into the thousands. In such instances, the computational problem that interested Kei Mori is of importance. The simple examples considered thus far have little computational interest.

[g]See M. S. Bartlett, *An Introduction to Stochastic Processes* (Cambridge University Press, Cambridge, 1955).

Let us express the general linear model of an economic system as

$$A(L)y_t + B(L)x_t = \Gamma(L)e_t \,. \tag{12}$$

In this equation system L is an operator

$$L^j y_t = y_{t-j}$$

y_t is an n-element vector of endogenous variables
x_t is an m-element vector of exogenous variables
e_t is an n-element vector of random errors.
$A(L)$, $B(L)$, $\Gamma(L)$ are matrix polynomials, i.e., each term is a finite polynomial in L.
$A(L)$ is square $(n \times n)$
$B(L)$ is rectangular $(n \times m)$
$\Gamma(L)$ is diagonal $(n \times n)$

$$A(L)y_t = \sum_{i=0}^{p} A_i y_{t-i} \,, \quad \text{and} \quad \det A_0 \not\approx 0 \,.$$

Equation system (12), consisting of n simultaneous stochastic and dynamic equations, represents the *structure* of an economic model. There are three other representations of the same system. They are

reduced form
final autoregressive form
solution form.

The beauty of the linear model is that all three representations can be expressed in closed form.

The reduced form expresses each endogenous variable as a function of prior values of all endogenous variables, all exogenous variables and all error terms in the system.

$$y_t = -A_0^{-1} \sum_{i=1}^{p} A_i y_{t-i} - A_0^{-1} \sum_{i=0}^{q} B_i x_{t-i} + A_0^{-1} \sum_{i=0}^{r} C_i e_{t-i} \tag{13}$$

The final autoregressive form can be written as

$$\begin{aligned} \|\Delta(L)\| y_t &= -a(L)B(L)x_t + a(L)\Gamma(L)e_t \\ \Delta(L) &= \text{det. } A(L) \\ a(L) &= \text{adjoint } A(L) \end{aligned} \tag{14}$$

$\|\Delta(L)\|$ is a diagonal matrix with $\Delta(L)$ in each diagonal element and zero elsewhere. This means that the l.h.s. is an autoregressive formula for each element of y_t and is the same in every case. This is a property of linear systems.

Equation (14) is the general expression for which I wrote out a numerical case in Eq. (10) above. It shows clearly that lag distributions in x_t and e_t are in the final autoregressive form, but these are not identical for each element of y_t.

The characteristic equation corresponding to (14) is

$$\Delta(L)y_{it} = 0 \qquad i = 1, 2, \dots, n. \tag{15}$$

If there are p lags in the system, the order of (15) will be at most np. Some lags may not be present in all equations. In any event, for $n = 100$ or more and p as great as 10 or 20, dependent on the time unit being used, the order can be very large — far different from the special cases under consideration in the preceding section. There can be a real problem in finding all the roots for a moderate size dynamic system.

The solution for y_t in this linear, dynamic, stochastic system takes the form

$$y_t = K\lambda^t - [A(L)]^{-1} B(L)x_t + [A(L)]^{-1} \Gamma(L)e_t \tag{16}$$

K = a matrix ($n \times np$) depending on the initial conditions of the system.

$$\lambda^t = \begin{pmatrix} \lambda_1^t \\ \lambda_2^t \\ \vdots \\ \lambda_{np}^t \end{pmatrix}$$

is a column vector of the (distinct) characteristic roots of the system.

It is useful to look at some other expressions for the solution in (16).

We could write

$$y_t = K\lambda^t - \frac{a(L)}{\Delta(L)}B(L)x_t + \frac{a(L)\Gamma(L)e_t}{\Delta(L)}. \tag{16$'$}$$

This is useful because it shows that the particular solution consists of rational polynomial lag distributions of x_t and e_t.

There are two other interesting expressions for writing the same solution. Equation (14) can be expressed as

$$\Delta(L)y_{it} = \varphi_i(t) \qquad i = 1, 2, \ldots, n, \tag{14$'$}$$

where $\varphi_i(t)$ is the r.h.s. of (14) for the ith element, (y_{it}), in y_t.

$$y_{it} = \frac{\varphi_i(t)}{\Delta(L)} = \prod_{j=1}^{np}(1 - \lambda_j L)^{-1}\varphi_i(t) \tag{14$''$}$$

It can also be expressed as[h]

$$y_{it} = \sum_{s=0}^{\infty}\sum_{j=1}^{np}\frac{\lambda_j^{s+np-1}}{\Pi_{j\neq k}(\lambda_j - \lambda_k)}\varphi_i(t-s). \tag{14$'''$}$$

It is assumed that the roots are distinct. In (14)$'''$, we have a generalization of the formula in (11), for the second-order case. This is interesting because it shows that if two roots are close together, there will be a tendency for y_{it} to be very large in absolute value; therefore in evaluating roots of a system, it is important to know something about their spacing as well as their absolute size.

The interesting feature of Eqs. (14)$''$ and (14)$'''$ is that all the terms of the complete solution of the linear, dynamic, stochastic system involve the characteristic roots, and these roots tell a great deal about the properties of the solution.

Statistical Properties of Characteristic Roots

From the expressions derived in closed form for the simple models, we can see clearly how the characteristic roots of a linear system depend on the structural parameters of the system. In the first-order case, the root is the coefficient of the lagged endogenous variable, which is either a fundamental parameter or a simple (ratio, e.g.) function of parameters. In the second-order case, the relationship between the roots and the parameters is given by the quadratic formula. This could be carried further in the cubic, quartic, or quintic case.

[h] K. S. Miller, "A note on stochastic difference equations," *Annals of Mathematical Statistics* **39**, 270–271 (1968).

But, in general, the coefficients in the final autoregressive form are functions of the structural parameters of the general linear model.

We now turn to the formulas (approximate) for the variance of roots as functions of the variances and covariances of the estimated structural parameters.

Asymptotic approximations for the variances and covariances of functions of random variables have been well-known for some time, and during the 1960s these were used for evaluating the variances and covariances needed for computation of the standard errors of forecast in linear econometric systems.[i] These kinds of approximations can also be used in nonlinear systems.

Among the several papers on standard errors of characteristic roots of a dynamic system, the formulas derived by Oberhofer and Kmenta are instructive.[j] They introduce a linear dynamic model with contemporaneous values of exogenous variables $x(t)$ and errors, $u(t)$. Their system is

$$\sum_{i=0}^{p} A_i y_{t-i} + B x_t = u_t \tag{17}$$

A_i are square $(n \times n)$ matrices of coefficients. The characteristic equation of this system can be expressed as

$$\det\left(\sum_{i=0}^{p} A_i \lambda^{p-i}\right) = 0 \tag{18}$$

$$\det\left(\sum_{i=0}^{p} A_i \lambda^{p-i}\right) = \sum_{j=0}^{n(p-1)} a_j \lambda^j = 0$$

$$\text{est. var } |\hat{\lambda}_K| = \sum \left(\frac{\partial|\lambda_K|}{\partial\hat{\alpha}_{cdi}} \frac{\partial|\lambda_K|}{\partial\hat{\alpha}_{efj}}\right) \text{ est. cov } \hat{\alpha}_{cdi}\hat{\alpha}_{efj} \tag{19}$$

$\hat{\alpha}_{cdi}$ is a typical term in A_i.

[i] A. S. Goldberger, A. L. Nagar, and H. S. Odeh, "The covariance matrices of reduced form coefficients and of forecasts for a structural econometric model," *Econometrica* **29**, 556–73 (1961).

[j] W. Oberhofer and J. Kmenta, "Estimation of standard errors of the characteristic roots of a dynamic econometric model," *Econometrica* **41**, 171–77 (January 1973).

The elements of A_i are estimated by standard econometric methods and are transformed by (19) in a quadratic form involving the derivatives of λ_K w.r.t. the structural parameters, evaluated at the point estimates.

Schmidt has shown that the formulas derived by Oberhofer and Kmenta are the same as those derived by a slightly different procedure by Theil and Boot.[k] They computed, for Klein Model I,

$$\text{est var } |\hat{\lambda}_1| = 0.0497$$

$$\text{S.E. } |\lambda_1| = 0.22$$

An alternative method for evaluating the variance (or other moment) of the distribution of characteristic roots would be to use some version of a Monte Carlo experiment. While this approach is lacking in generality it has the advantage of being applicable in finite samples, of the size often used in econometric investigations.

In a system such as (17), random drawings are selected from a normal probability distribution having the same variance covariance matrix of u_t as that estimated by a sample, which is also used to estimate A_i and B. For a given data matrix of x_t $(t = 1, 2, \ldots T)$ and given initial conditions for y_t, *which are both kept fixed in replications of the drawings of random numbers for* u_t, we can generate solutions for y_t. The solution from the ith replication will be denoted as $y_t^{(i)}$ $(t = 1, 2, \ldots, T)$. The values $y_t^{(i)}$ and x_t $(t = 1, 2, \ldots, T)$ constitute a pseudo-sample of observations. For each replicated pseudo-sample there will be a set of parameter estimates, denoted as $A_i^{(j)}$, $B^{(j)}$ (jth replication). This provides us with a replicated set of estimated models. Each model will produce np roots; these can be ordered, and formed into frequency distributions for each root — the largest, next largest, etc. The computed variance of the frequency distribution of any root is an estimate, by Monte Carlo techniques, of var $|\hat{\lambda}_i|$. In addition to providing a finite sample estimate of the variance this method does not have to make linear approximations to the function relating elements of λ to elements of A_i and B.

[k] Peter Schmidt, "The algebraic equivalence of the Oberhofer–Kmenta and Theil–Boot formulae for the asymptotic variance of the characteristic roots of a dynamic econometric model," *Econometrica* **42**, 591–92 (May 1974). See H. Theil and J. C. G. Boot fn. f, above. See also H. Neudecker and C. van de Panne, "Note on the asymptotic standard errors of latent roots of econometric equation systems," *Review of the International Statistical Institute* **34**, 43–47 (1966).

Nonlinear Systems

Characteristic roots are defined for linear models, even though the relationship between λ and the basic parameters of the model is highly nonlinear. Most econometric models are nonlinear in their original specification. There are fundamental reasons for this, having to do with accounting identities and convexities in behavior or structural constraints (production functions, e.g.).

What is the meaning of characteristic roots of a nonlinear equation system? One meaning is to associate the roots of the corresponding linear approximation to the nonlinear structure, *in the neighborhood of some point in space.* There will not, in general, be one vector of characteristic roots of a nonlinear system, but we may make linear approximations in the neighborhood of key points and study the characteristic roots for each system of linear approximations.

An interesting case in the literature of business-cycle analysis is the nonlinear model of Kaldor.[1] This model has a particular nonlinear structure that is capable of leading the system to a limit cycle — a repeated oscillation without dampening. In linear theory, complex roots — which are capable of generating a cycle — are either damped, in a limit cycle, or explosive, depending on whether the largest characteristic root

$$|\lambda| \lesseqgtr -1$$

Allowing for trend, and expressing the linear system as *deviations* from trend, we would reject

$$|\lambda| \geq 1$$

because we generally do not observe explosive cycles, and because linear systems with

$$|\lambda| = 1$$

will have increasing variance over time, in a stochastic mode. (See notes c, d, e above).

The Kaldor model has the general shape depicted in Fig. 1.

[1]Nicholas Kaldor, "A model of the trade cycle," *Economic Journal* L (March 1940), 78–92.

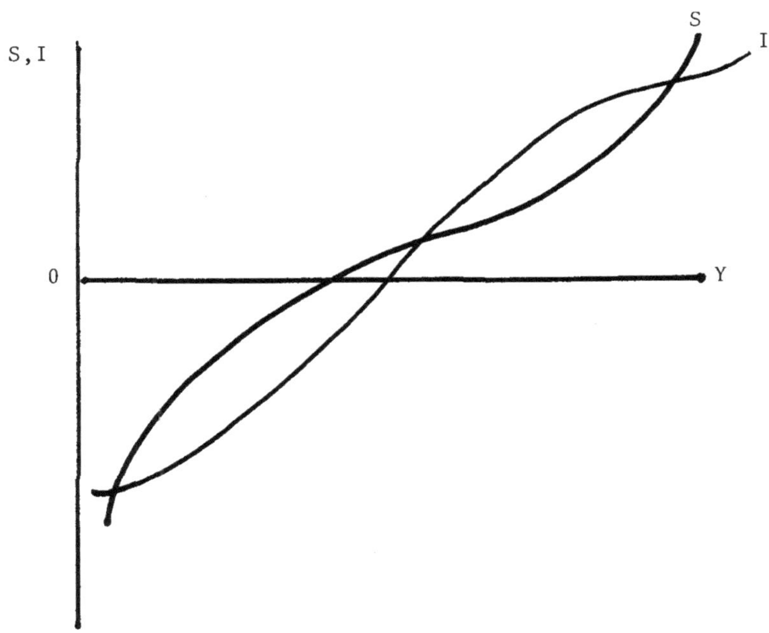

Fig. 1. The Kaldor model.

The nonlinear equations are

$S_t = S(Y_t)$	savings function	(20)
$I_t = I(Y_t,\, K_{t-1})$	investment function	(21)
$Y_t - Y_{t-1} = Y(I_t - S_t)$	output adjustment	(22)
$K_t - K_{t-1} = I_t$	definition of capital stock.	(23)

S_t = savings

Y_t = total income or product

I_t = net investment

K_t = stock of capital

In order to generate a limit cycle, this model must show three intersection points, two being stable (marginal propensity to save exceeding the marginal propensity to invest), and one being unstable. The latter must occur between the other two. Also, the left tangency point between a shifting investment curve and a steady savings curve at the left equilibrium point should be in a negative portion of the diagram.

Stability in this nonlinear system can easily be determined in two dimensions by comparing (visually, if desired) the slopes of the two curves to see if

$$dS/dY > \partial I/\partial Y\,.$$

This inequality should hold for the two extreme equilibrium points, at the right and at the left. We must have

$$\frac{dS}{dY} < \frac{\partial I}{\partial Y}$$

at the middle equilibrium point.

Characteristic root analysis could be used in the sense of approximating the system, linearly, in the neighborhood of the right and left equilibrium points to see if

$$|\lambda_i| < 1$$

for each linear approximation.

The method of stochastic simulation could also be used for stability analysis in this case. Equations (20), (21), and (22) could each be disturbed by terms from random drawings. This has been done in replicated drawings for a parametric version of the Kaldor system. A limit cycle was generated and the variance of the solution was tabulated across replicated drawings. The result was that the numerically generated variances of the solution stabilized; they did not tend to grow indefinitely.[m] This result was generalized by Kosobud and O'Neill. They demonstrated asymptotic orbital stability in a stochastic sense, for the Kaldor type of model.[n]

Characteristic root analysis can be used, locally, for study of larger, more complicated nonlinear models but stochastic simulation and more general analysis of the type used by Kosobud and O'Neill would be more appropriate, yet

[m] L. R. Klein and R. S. Preston, "Stochastic nonlinear models," *Econometrica* **37**, 95–106 (January 1969).

[n] R. F. Kosobud and W. D. O'Neill, "Stochastic implications of orbital asymptotic stability of a nonlinear trade cycle model," *Econometrica* **40**, 69–86 (January 1972).

the root structure of dynamic models provides interesting ways of describing system properties.

References

1. M. S. Bartlett, *An Introduction to Stochastic Processes* (Cambridge University Press, Cambridge, 1955).
2. A. S. Goldberger, A. L. Nagar, and H. S. Odeh, "The covariance matrices of reduced form coefficients and of forecasts for a structural econometric model," *Econometrica* vol. **29**, 556–73 (1961).
3. Nicholas Kaldor, "A model of the trade cycle," *Economic Journal* vol. **L**, 78–92 (March 1940).
4. M. Kalecki, "On the Gibrat distribution," *Econometrica* vol. **13**, 161–70 (1945).
5. L. R. Klein and R. S. Preston, "Stochastic nonlinear models," *Econometrica* vol. **37**, 95–106 (January 1969).
6. R. F. Kosobud and W. D. O'Neill, "Stochastic implications of orbital asymptotic stability of a nonlinear trade cycle model," *Econometrica* vol. **40**, 69–86 (January 1972).
7. Edwin Kuh, John W. Neese, and Peter Hollinger, *Structural Sensitivity in Econometric Models* (John Wiley & Sons, New York, 1985), pp. 72 ff.
8. Youcai Liang and Lawrence R. Klein, "The two-gap paradigm in the Chinese case: A pedagogical exercise," *China Economic Review*, vol. **I**, 1–8 (Spring 1989).
9. H. B. Mann and A. Wald, "On the statistical treatment of linear stochastic difference equations," *Econometrica* vol. **11**, 173–220 (July-October, 1943).
10. K. S. Miller, "A note on stochastic difference equations," *Annals of Mathematical Statistics* vol. **39**, 270–271 (1968).
11. H. Neudecker and C. van de Panne, "Note on the asymptotic standard errors of latent roots of econometric equation systems," *Review of the International Statistical Institute* vol. **34**, 43–47 (1966).
12. W. Oberhofer and J. Kmenta, "Estimation of standard errors of the characteristic roots of a dynamic econometric model," *Econometrica* vol. **41**, 171–77 (January 1973).
13. P. A. Samuelson, *Foundations of Economic Analysis* (Harvard University Press, Cambridge, 1947).
14. Peter Schmidt, "The algebraic equivalence of the Oberhofer–Kmenta and Theil–Boot formulae for the asymptotic variance of the characteristic roots of a dynamic econometric model," *Econometrica* vol. **42**, 591–92 (May 1974).
15. H. Theil and J. C. G. Boot, "The final form of econometric equation systems," *Review of the International Statistical Institute* vol. **30**, 136–52 (1962).

COMMENTS ON LAWRENCE KLEIN'S "THE ROLE OF CHARACTERISTIC ROOTS IN DYNAMIC ECONOMIC MODELS"

AKIRA ONISHI
Soka University

When I was a graduate student at Keio University, Kei was a very intimate friend of mine. During those days he was interested in studying trade cycle phenomena using a Goodwin type nonlinear investment function. I had opportunities to discuss with him about the topic of the role of characteristic roots in dynamic economic systems, since my major was to develop a trade cycle theory following J. R. Hicks' "A contribution to the theory of the trade cycle." Kei showed me his dynamic simulation rsults using a nonlinear investment function in a macroeconomic system. I was rather surprised to see that he made some pioneering efforts forming dynamic simulations of a macroeconomic model, using a large-scale computer. Because of very expensive computing costs at those times, it was incredible for me to apply such an advanced technology in a study on a trade cycle model. Since then Kei successfully developed much more sophisticated quarterly models of the Japanese economy in discussing the topics of the role of characteristic roots in dynamic economic systems. He tried to explain trade cycles of the Japanese economy for the period, 1953–1961 using computer simulations.

In this volume Prof. Klein presented his excellent paper on "The role of characteristic roots in dynamic economic systems" where he explained about dynamic properties of coefficient matrices with regard to both endogenous and exogenous variable vectors, together with random error vectors. I would fully agree with his presentation. In order to ascertain the dynamic properties of economic models, there are two approaches; one is to study theoretically the role and importance of characteristic roots in dynamic economic models, and the other is to make use of dynamic simulation testing of these models using computers. In the case of linear dynamic economic systems, it is not very difficult to find out about mathematical properties of the characteristic roots in the models. On the other hand, it is rather difficult simply to apply such a theoretical method in the case of large-scale nonlinear dynamic economic models like global economic models. We therefore largely depend upon the sophisticated computer simulations, thanks to the recent advancement of computer technologies in both hardware and software.

In order to carry out my responsibility as discussant, I would like to present a dynamic simulation result of the Japanese economy in a global perspective starting in 1993 and continuing to 2000, using the latest FUGI global model 7.0, M80. This is an outcome of my earlier discussions with Kei on global economic models which are still on the frontiers of econometric research.

A listing of available variables in FUGI is followed by simulated GDP growth rates for individual countries and regions.

****
INDEX OF WORLD TABLE
****

1	MAJOR ECONOMIC INDICATOR	
2	GDP#	- GROSS DOMESTIC PRODUCT (CONST.) (AVERAGE PERCENTAGE CHANGES)
3	NP	- NUMBER OF POPULATION (AVERAGE PERCENTAGE CHANGES)
4	NP	- NUMBER OF POPULATION
5	LCLF	- CIVILIAN LABOR FORCE (AVERAGE PERCENTAGE CHANGES)
6	LCLF	- CIVILIAN LABOR FORCE
7	CEMP	- CIVILIAN EMPLOYMENT (AVERAGE PERCENTAGE CHANGES)
8	CEMP	- CIVILIAN EMPLOYMENT
9	UNEMPR	- UMEMPLOYMENT RATE
10	LPI	- LABOR PRODUCTIVITY INDEX (AVERAGE PERCENTAGE CHANGES)
11	LPI	- LABOR PRODUCTIVITY INDEX
12	GDP#/CEMP	- LABOUR PRODUCTIVITY
13	WSEI/CPI	- REAL WAGE RATE PER EMPLOYEE (AVERAGE PERCENTAGE CHANGES)
14	WSEI	- NOMINAL WAGE RATE PER EMPLOYEE (AVERAGE PERCENTAGE CHANGES)
15	CPI	- CONSUMER PRICE INDEX (AVERAGE PERCENTAGE CHANGES)
16	WPI	- WHOLESALE PRICE INDEX (AVERAGE PERCENTAGE CHANGES)
17	PE	- EXPORT UNIT VALUE INDEX (AVERAGE PERCENTAGE CHANGES)
18	PES	- UNIT VALUE INDEX OF EXPORTS (IN TERMS OF US DOLLAR) (AVERAGE PERCENTAGE CHANGES)
19	PM	- IMPORT UNIT VALUE INDEX (AVERAGE PERCENTAGE CHANGES)
20	PMS	- UNIT VALUE INDEX OF IMPORTS (IN TERMS OF US DOLLAR) (AVERAGE PERCENTAGE CHANGES)
21	FERSI	- FOREIGN EXCHANGE RATE INDEX (PER US DOLLAR) (AVERAGE PERCENTAGE CHANGES)
22	FERSI	- FOREIGN EXCHANGE RATE INDEX (PER US DOLLAR)
23	FERS	- FOREIGN EXCHANGE RATE (PER US DOLLAR)
24	M1	- MONEY SUPPLY (M1), OUTSTANDING (AVERAGE PERCENTAGE CHANGES)
25	M2	- MONEY AND QUASI-MONEY (M1+MTD), OUTSTANDING (AVERAGE PERCENTAGE CHANGES)
26	IV#	- MONEY SUPPLY - CONSTANT INCOME INDEX (AVERAGE PERCENTAGE CHANGES)
27	IN	- CENTRAL BANK'S OFFICIAL DISCOUNT RATE
28	IP	- PRIME RATE
29	IC	- CALL MONEY RATE, FEDERAL FUND RATE
30	IB	- GOVERNMENT BOND YIELD ; LONG-TERM
31	GE	- TOTAL GOVERNMENT EXPENDITURE (AVERAGE PERCENTAGE CHANGES)
32	GE/GDP	- GOVERNMENT EXPENDITURE / NOMINAL GDP
33	R	- CURRENT REVENUE (CUR.) (AVERAGE PERCENTAGE CHANGES)
34	R/GDP	- CURRENT REVENUE / NOMINAL GDP
35	GDOS	- GOVERNMENT DEFICIT OR SURPLUS
36	GDOS/GDPS	- GOVERNMENT DEFICIT SURPLUS / NOMINAL GDP IN TERMS OF CURRENT US DOLLAR
37	GSW#/GDP#	- GOVERNMENT EXPENDITURE ON SOCIAL SECURITY & WELFARE (CONST.) / GROSS DOMESTIC PRODUCT (CONST.)
38	GH#/GDP#	- GOVERNMENT HEALTH EXPENDITURE (CONST.) / GROSS DOMESTIC PRODUCT (CONST.)
39	GED#/GDP#	- GOVERNMENT EDUCATION EXPENDITURE (CONST.) / GROSS DOMESTIC PRODUCT (CONST.)
40	GDF/GDP	- GOVERNMENT DEFENSE EXPENDITURE / NOMINAL GDP
41	ETFOB	- MERCHANDISE ; EXPORTS (F.O.B.) (AVERAGE PERCENTAGE CHANGES)
42	MTFOB	- MERCHANDISE ; IMPORTS (F.O.B.) (AVERAGE PERCENTAGE CHANGES)

43	ETFOB#	- MERCHANDISE EXPORTS(FOB) AT CONSTANTS US DOLLARS (AVERAGE PERCENTAGE CHANGES)
44	MTFOB#	- MERCHANDISE,IMPORTS(FOB) AT CONSTANT PRICES (AVERAGE PERCENTAGE CHANGES)
45	ETFOB	- MERCHANDISE ; EXPORTS (F.O.B.)
46	MTFOB	- MERCHANDISE ; IMPORTS (F.O.B.)
47	TB	- TRADE BALANCE (F.O.B.)
48	EMFOB	- (AVERAGE PERCENTAGE CHANGES)
49	MMFOB	- (AVERAGE PERCENTAGE CHANGES)
50	EMFOB	-
51	MMFOB	-
52	TBB	-
53	SC	- OTHER GOODS, SERVICES AND INCOME ; CREDIT
54	SD	- OTHER GOODS, SERVICES AND INCOME ; DEBIT
55	CBP	- CURRENT BALANCE OF PAYMENTS
56	CBP/GDPS	- CURRENT BALANCE OF PAYMENTS / NOMINAL GDP IN TERMS OF CURRENT US DOLLAR
57	DIL	- DIRECT INVESTMENT IN COUNTRY
58	DIA	- DIRECT INVESTMENT ABROAD
59	POINL	- PORTFOLIO INVESTMENT ; LIABILITIES
60	POINA	- PORTFOLIO INVESTMENT ; ASSETS
61	LTCB	- LONG-TERM CAPITAL BALANCE
62	BBP	- BASIC BALANCE OF PAYMENT
63	BBP/GDPS	- BASIC BALANCE OF PAYMENTS / NOMINAL GDP IN TERMS OF CURRENT US DOLLAR
64	PES/PMS	- TERMS OF TRADE (AVERAGE PERCENTAGE CHANGES)
65	PES/PMS	- TERMS OF TRADE
66	GDP#/NP	- REAL GDP PER CAPITA (AVERAGE PERCENTAGE CHANGES)
67	GDPS/NP	- GDPS PER CAPITA (AVERAGE PERCENTAGE CHANGES)
68	GDP#/NP	- REAL GDP PER CAPITA
69	GDPS/NP	- GDPS PER CAPITA
70	IPCID	- CHANGES IN PER CAPITA INCOME GAP ; AVERAGE PER CAPITA INCOME OF WHOLE DME = 1
71	IPCID	- CHANGES IN PER CAPITA INCOME GAP ; AVERAGE PER CAPITA INCOME OF WHOLE AME = 100
72	IPCID	- CHANGES IN PER CAPITA INCOME GAP ; AVERAGE PER CAPITA INCOME OF WHOLE WRD = 100
73	GDPE*COMP	- ANNUAL AVERAGE GROWTH RATES OF REAL GDP EXPENDITURE COMPONENTS
74	SOEAM	- SHARE OF EXPORTS TO DME AND SHARE OF IMPORTS FROM DME (CURRENT US DOLLAR)
75	SOEAM	- SHARE OF EXPORTS TO DME AND SHARE OF IMPORTS FROM DME (CONST.)
76	SORGC	- SHARE OF REAL GDP COMPONENTS
77	SECGDP	- ANNUAL AVERAGE GROWTH RATES OF SECTRAL REAL GDP
78	SECGDP	- SHARE OF SECTRAL REAL GDP
79	ODA	- TOTAL OFFICIAL DEVELOPMENT ASSISTANCE TO DEVELOPING COUNTRIES (NET, CURRENT US DOLLAR)
80	ODA/GDPS	- ODA AS PERCENTAGE OF GDP (BASED ON CURRENT US DOLLAR)
81	ODAB	- BILATERAL OFFICIAL DEVELOPMENT ASSISTANCE TO DEVELOPING COUNTRIES (NET, CURRENT US DOLLAR)
82	ODAM	- CONTRIBUTIONS TO MULTILATERAL INSTITUTIONS (NET, CURRENT US DOLLAR)
83	ODABR	- ODAB RECEIVED
84	AM	- ODA RECEIVED FROM MULTILATERAL INSTITUTIONS
85	PFDI	- EACH DEVELOPED COUNTRY'S FOREIGN DIRECT INVESTMENT TO DEVELOPING COUNTRIES
86	PFDIR	- PFDI RECEIVED FROM DEVELOPED COUNTRIES
87	DOD	- PUBLIC DEBT OUTSTANDING (LONG TERM) ; ALL CREDITORS
88	DISB	- PUBLIC DISBURSEMENTS (LONG TERM) ; ALL CREDITORS
89	TDS	- PUBLIC TOTAL DEBT SERVICE (LONG TERM) ; ALL CREDITORS

90	INT	- PUBLIC INTEREST PAYMENTS (LONG TERM) ; ALL CREDITORS
91	PREP	- PUBLIC PRINCIPAL REPAYMENTS (LONG TERM) ; ALL CREDITORS
92	INTOC	- PUBLIC AVERAGE RATE OF INTEREST PAID (LONG TERM) ; ALL CREDITORS
93	DSR	- PUBLIC DEBT SERVICE RATIO (LONG TERM)
94	DER	- PUBLIC DEBT OUTSTANDING/EXPORTS RATIO (LONG TERM)
95	DGR	- PUBLIC DEBT OUTSTANDING/GDPS RATIO (LONG TERM)
96	EDT	- PUBLIC DEBT OUTSTANDING
97	DSRLT	- DEBT SERVICE RATIO
98	DERT	- DEBT OUTSTANDING/EXPORTS RATIO
99	DGRT	- DEBT OUTSTANDING/GDPS RATIO
100	GDP#	- GROSS DOMESTIC PRODUCT (CONST.)
101	CP#	- PRIVATE FINAL CONSUMPTION EXPENDITURE (CONST.)
102	CG#	- GOVERNMENT FINAL CONSUMPTION EXPENDITURE (CONST.)
103	NHI#	- NON-HOUSING INVESTMENT (CONST.)
104	HI#	- HOUSING INVESTMENT (CONST.)
105	IIS#	- INCREASE IN STOCKS (CONST.)
106	E#	- EXPORTS OF GOODS AND SERVICES (CONST.)
107	M#	- IMPORTS OF GOODS AND SERVICES (CONST.)
108	GDPS	- GROSS DOMESTIC PRODUCT (CURRENT U.S. DOLLAR)
109	GDP#	- GROSS DOMESTIC PRODUCT (CONST.) (AVERAGE PERCENTAGE CHANGES)
110	CP#	- PRIVATE FINAL CONSUMPTION EXPENDITURE (CONST.) (AVERAGE PERCENTAGE CHANGES)
111	CG#	- GOVERNMENT FINAL CONSUMPTION EXPENDITURE (CONST.) (AVERAGE PERCENTAGE CHANGES)
112	NHI#	- NON-HOUSING INVESTMENT (CONST.) (AVERAGE PERCENTAGE CHANGES)
113	HI#	- HOUSING INVESTMENT (CONST.) (AVERAGE PERCENTAGE CHANGES)
114	IIS#	- INCREASE IN STOCKS (CONST.) (AVERAGE PERCENTAGE CHANGES)
115	E#	- EXPORTS OF GOODS AND SERVICES (CONST.) (AVERAGE PERCENTAGE CHANGES)
116	M#	- IMPORTS OF GOODS AND SERVICES (CONST.) (AVERAGE PERCENTAGE CHANGES)
117	GDPS	- GROSS DOMESTIC PRODUCT (CURRENT U.S. DOLLAR) (AVERAGE PERCENTAGE CHANGES)
118	PGDP	- IMPLICIT DEFLATOR OF GDP (AVERAGE PERCENTAGE CHANGES)
119	PCP	- IMPLICIT DEFLATOR OF PRIVATE CONSUMPTION EXPENDITURE (AVERAGE PERCENTAGE CHANGES)
120	PCG	- IMPLICIT DEFLATOR OF GOVERNMENT CONSUMPTION EXPENDITURE (AVERAGE PERCENTAGE CHANGES)
121	PNHI	- IMPLICIT DEFLATOR OF NON-HOUSING INVESTMENT (AVERAGE PERCENTAGE CHANGES)
122	PHI	- IMPLICIT DEFLATOR OF HOUSING INVESTMENT (AVERAGE PERCENTAGE CHANGES)
123	PENA	- IMPLICIT DEFLATOR OF EXPORTS OF GOODS AND SERVICES (AVERAGE PERCENTAGE CHANGES)
124	PMNA	- IMPLICIT DEFLATOR OF IMPORTS OF GOODS AND SERVICES (AVERAGE PERCENTAGE CHANGES)
125	GDP	- GROSS DOMESTIC PRODUCT (CUR.)
126	GDP	- GROSS DOMESTIC PRODUCT (CUR.) (AVERAGE PERCENTAGE CHANGES)
127	GDPS/GDPS<SUM>	- SHARE OF NOMINAL GDP IN TERMS OF CURRENT US DOLLAR IN THE WORLD
128	GDP#/GDP#<SUM>	- SHARE OF REAL GDP (CONST.) IN THE WORLD
129	ETFOB/EW	- SHARE OF EXPORT IN THE WORLD
130	MTFOB/MW	- SHARE OF IMPORT IN THE WORLD
131	OIL	- OIL REQUIREMENT (AVERAGE PERCENTAGE CHANGES)
132	COAL	- COAL REQUIREMENT (AVERAGE PERCENTAGE CHANGES)
133	GAS	- NATURAL GAS REQUIREMENT (AVERAGE PERCENTAGE CHANGES)
134	FOSSIL	- FOSSIL ENERGY IN TERMS OF METRIC TON(OIL EQUIVALENT) (AVERAGE PERCENTAGE CHANGES)
135	ALTENGY	- ALTERNATIVE ENERGY SUPPLY(METRIC TON) (AVERAGE PERCENTAGE CHANGES)
136	ENGYR	- ENERGY REQUIREMENTS(METRIC TON OIL EQUIVALENT) (AVERAGE PERCENTAGE CHANGES)

137 OIL - OIL REQUIREMENT
138 COAL - COAL REQUIREMENT
139 GAS - NATURAL GAS REQUIREMENT
140 FOSSIL - FOSSIL ENERGY IN TERMS OF METRIC TON(OIL EQUIVALENT)
141 ALTENGY - ALTERNATIVE ENERGY SUPPLY(METRIC TON)
142 ENGYR - ENERGY REQUIREMENTS(METRIC TON OIL EQUIVALENT)
143 EPC - ENERGY REQUIREMENTS PER CAPITA
144 ALTENGYR - ALTERNATIVE ENERGY RATIO TO TOTAL ENERGY
145 ESR - ENERGY SAVINGS RATE TO GDP# IN TERMS OF ENERGY INTENSITY
146 AETR - ALTERNATIVE ENERGY TECHNOLOGY RATE IN TERMS OF CO2 EFFICIENCY
147 CO2EMN - CO2 EMISSION FROM FOSSIL ENERGY USE (AVERAGE PERCENTAGE CHANGES)
148 CO2EMN - CO2 EMISSION FROM FOSSIL ENERGY USE
149 CO2PC - CO2 EMISSION PER CAPITA (AVERAGE PERCENTAGE CHANGES)
150 CO2PC - CO2 EMISSION PER CAPITA
151 SOX - SOX EMISSION (AVERAGE PERCENTAGE CHANGES)
152 SOX - SOX EMISSION
153 NOX - NOX EMISSION (AVERAGE PERCENTAGE CHANGES)
154 NOX - NOX EMISSION
155 CH4 - METHANE GAS EMISSION (AVERAGE PERCENTAGE CHANGES)
156 CH4 - METHANE GAS EMISSION
157 BIRTHR - BIRTH RATE
158 DEATHR - DEATH RATE
159 LIFEEXP - LIFE EXPECTANCY AT BIRTH
160 NPM - NUMBER OF POPULATION:MALE
161 NPF - NUMBER OF POPULATION:FEMALE
162 NPMEA - NUMBER OF POPULATION FROM 15 TO 64 YEARS:MALE
163 NPFEA - NUMBER OF POPULATION FROM 15 TO 64 YEARS: FEMALE
164 NPMO65 - NUMBER OF POPULATION OVER 65 YEARS:MALE
165 NPFO65 - NUMBER OF POPULATION OVER 65 YEARS: FEMALE
166 NPURBAN/NP - URBAN POPULATION RATIO
167 DP - DISPLACED PERSONS
168 DPR - DISPLACED PERSONS , RECEIVED

UNIT :

MD - MILLIONS OF 1985 US DOLLARS
MD85 - MILLIONS OF 1985 US DOLLARS AT 1985 CONSTANT PRICES
MDS - MILLIONS OF CURRENT US DOLLARS
USD - 1985 US DOLLAR
USDS - CURRENT US DOLLAR
85=100 - INDEX NUMBER
% - PERCENTAGE
TP - THOUSANDS OF PERSONS

```
+-------------------+
:  WORLD TABLE -   2 :
+-------------------+
```

GDP#   - GROSS DOMESTIC PRODUCT (CONST.) (AVERAGE PERCENTAGE CHANGES)

UNIT : %

- MEDIUM TERM -	81-90	1990	1991	1992	1993	1994	1995	1996	1997	1998	1999	2000	91-00
World Total	2.9	2.1	.7	1.6	1.8	2.9	3.1	2.7	2.9	3.3	3.2	3.2	2.5
OECD	2.8	2.1	.5	1.8	1.5	2.5	2.7	2.1	2.4	2.8	2.7	2.6	2.1
The Major Seven	2.8	2.0	.4	1.8	1.6	2.4	2.7	2.1	2.4	2.8	2.8	2.6	2.2
Developed Market Economies	2.8	2.0	.5	1.7	1.4	2.4	2.6	2.0	2.3	2.7	2.6	2.5	2.1
Developed Asia-Pacific	4.0	4.2	3.6	1.5	.5	1.9	2.9	2.8	4.0	4.5	4.5	3.8	3.0
Japan	4.1	4.8	4.0	1.3	.1	1.6	3.1	3.0	4.3	4.9	4.8	4.0	3.1
North America	2.7	.7	-1.2	2.4	2.8	3.1	2.7	1.6	1.9	2.3	2.3	2.2	2.0
United States	2.7	.8	-1.1	2.5	2.8	3.1	2.6	1.5	1.8	2.3	2.2	2.2	2.0
EU	2.3	2.7	1.2	1.0	-.1	1.6	2.4	2.2	2.0	2.2	2.1	2.2	1.7
Other Western Europe	2.1	2.2	-.1	1.3	.8	1.4	1.3	1.4	1.5	1.5	1.5	1.5	1.2
Developing Economies	3.8	4.9	4.0	5.5	5.5	4.9	4.8	4.8	4.9	5.0	5.1	5.1	4.9
Oil Exporting Countries	2.2	5.7	3.0	5.4	4.4	3.5	3.6	3.8	3.9	4.1	4.2	4.3	4.0
OPEC	2.2	6.2	2.7	6.4	4.5	3.1	3.3	3.4	3.4	3.5	3.6	3.6	3.7
Non Oil Exporting Countries	4.9	4.4	4.5	5.5	6.1	5.8	5.4	5.4	5.4	5.5	5.5	5.5	5.5
NIES	3.9	3.1	4.5	2.6	4.1	4.5	4.8	4.9	5.0	5.1	5.2	5.4	4.6
Asian NIES	8.4	8.4	7.8	5.2	5.7	6.3	6.8	6.8	6.8	6.8	6.8	6.8	6.6
Latin American NIES	1.6	-.5	2.1	.6	2.8	3.0	3.1	3.2	3.4	3.6	3.7	3.9	2.9
Asia-Pacific	7.1	7.1	5.6	7.2	7.6	7.2	6.8	6.8	6.8	6.8	6.8	6.8	6.8
East Asia	8.7	7.7	7.2	9.3	9.8	8.5	7.4	7.3	7.2	7.1	7.0	6.9	7.7
China	9.1	7.4	6.9	12.8	13.0	10.0	7.9	7.6	7.4	7.2	7.1	6.9	8.7
ASEAN	5.5	7.6	6.2	5.7	6.5	6.8	7.0	7.1	7.2	7.2	7.3	7.3	6.8
Other Southeast Asia	3.2	2.6	2.1	3.7	6.8	7.0	7.7	8.2	8.6	7.9	7.3	7.2	6.6
Southwest Asia	5.7	5.7	2.0	4.1	3.7	4.8	5.2	5.3	5.4	5.9	6.1	6.4	4.9
Pacific Islands	1.6	.0	6.0	1.6	2.0	2.0	2.0	2.0	2.0	2.0	2.0	2.0	2.3
Middle East	2.5	6.8	.9	7.7	5.1	3.4	3.2	3.3	3.3	3.2	3.2	3.2	3.7
Africa	1.5	3.1	2.1	2.2	1.7	1.7	1.8	1.9	1.9	2.0	2.0	2.0	1.9
North Africa	1.4	1.1	1.0	2.3	2.3	2.3	2.3	2.2	2.3	2.3	2.3	2.3	2.2
Sub-Saharan Africa	1.6	4.5	2.9	2.2	1.4	1.4	1.5	1.6	1.7	1.8	1.8	1.8	1.8
Latin America and Caribbean	1.2	.7	3.7	2.7	3.4	2.6	2.7	2.7	2.8	3.0	3.1	3.2	3.0
Mediterranean	4.6	4.4	4.2	3.2	4.5	4.5	4.5	4.5	4.5	4.5	4.4	4.4	4.3

Economies in Transition	1.7	-5.3	-8.7	-15.5	-10.3	-.9	2.0	1.8	1.9	2.0	2.0	2.0	-2.6
Eastern Europe	.6	-10.4	-11.6	-5.6	-.6	1.8	2.6	2.0	1.9	1.8	1.8	1.7	-.5
Former USSR	2.0	-4.0	-8.0	-17.8	-12.8	-1.7	1.8	1.8	1.9	2.0	2.0	2.1	-3.1
1 Japan	4.1	4.8	4.0	1.3	.1	1.6	3.1	3.0	4.3	4.9	4.8	4.0	3.1
2 Australia	3.0	-.5	.4	2.5	3.2	4.0	1.5	1.4	1.5	1.6	1.7	1.8	2.0
3 New Zealand	1.8	-.4	-1.6	1.4	4.6	5.0	1.6	1.4	1.4	1.4	1.4	1.4	1.8
4 Canada	2.9	-.5	-1.8	.7	2.9	3.1	3.6	2.7	2.1	2.5	2.7	2.6	2.1
5 United States	2.7	.8	-1.1	2.5	2.8	3.1	2.6	1.5	1.8	2.3	2.2	2.2	2.0
6 Belgium-Luxembourg	2.0	3.4	1.9	1.0	.9	1.9	1.9	.5	.8	1.1	.9	.8	1.2
7 Denmark	2.1	2.0	1.2	1.2	1.2	1.7	2.1	1.6	1.5	1.4	1.2	1.1	1.4
8 France	2.3	2.2	1.2	1.3	-.8	1.1	2.8	1.8	1.8	1.7	1.6	1.4	1.4
9 Germany,Fed.Rep.	2.1	5.1	3.7	2.0	-.8	1.5	2.4	2.6	1.9	2.4	1.9	2.1	2.0
10 Greece	1.5	-.1	1.8	1.0	1.3	1.8	2.5	2.7	2.8	2.8	2.7	2.7	2.2
11 Ireland	3.7	8.3	2.5	1.7	1.2	2.4	3.5	3.6	2.3	1.3	.8	.6	2.0
12 Italy	2.2	2.2	1.4	1.1	.3	1.8	2.2	2.2	2.1	2.1	2.0	1.9	1.7
13 Netherlands	1.9	3.9	2.2	1.3	-.3	1.1	1.3	1.4	1.2	1.4	1.7	1.7	1.3
14 United Kingdom	2.6	.5	-2.2	-.6	1.8	2.3	2.5	3.2	3.4	3.6	4.1	4.5	2.2
15 Portugal	2.7	4.4	2.1	.8	.4	1.2	2.5	1.3	1.1	1.0	1.3	1.5	1.3
16 Spain	3.0	3.7	2.3	1.0	-.7	1.7	2.5	1.9	1.4	1.2	1.2	1.1	1.4
17 Austria	2.2	4.6	3.0	1.6	-.1	2.1	1.5	1.2	1.5	1.6	1.5	1.6	1.6
18 Finland	3.2	.3	-6.4	-2.6	-1.6	1.9	1.8	1.8	1.9	1.9	1.8	1.8	.2
19 Iceland	2.7	.4	1.4	1.3	1.1	2.9	2.6	2.6	2.7	2.7	2.7	2.6	2.3
20 Norway	2.5	1.7	1.6	1.9	1.5	1.6	2.7	1.3	1.5	1.4	1.6	1.5	1.7
21 Sweden	2.0	.7	-1.8	-.7	-1.7	1.7	1.6	1.6	1.6	1.6	1.6	1.5	.7
22 Switzerland	2.1	2.3	-.1	1.3	.8	1.4	1.2	1.4	1.4	1.5	1.5	1.5	1.2
23 China	9.1	7.4	6.9	12.8	13.0	10.0	7.9	7.6	7.4	7.2	7.1	6.9	8.7
24 Hong Kong & Macau	7.2	7.8	7.2	5.0	6.0	5.6	6.6	6.7	6.9	7.1	7.2	7.4	6.6
25 Taiwan,Province of China	8.0	7.8	7.2	6.2	6.7	6.3	6.3	6.5	6.8	7.0	7.3	7.6	6.8
26 Korea,Republic of	9.3	9.2	8.5	4.5	4.6	6.5	7.5	7.3	7.1	6.9	6.7	6.5	6.6
27 N.Korea	4.3	4.1	3.7	-5.0	-3.0	2.5	2.5	2.4	2.3	2.3	2.3	2.3	1.2
28 Indonesia	5.6	7.1	6.6	6.1	6.3	6.4	7.5	7.7	7.7	7.7	7.8	7.8	7.2
29 Malaysia	6.0	9.8	7.0	6.5	7.6	8.3	7.9	8.4	8.6	8.8	9.0	8.9	8.1
30 Philippines	1.6	2.7	-.6	.0	1.8	4.2	3.5	3.7	3.7	3.9	4.0	4.1	2.8
31 Singapore	7.0	8.1	6.7	5.8	8.3	6.3	5.4	5.1	4.9	4.7	4.5	4.4	5.6
32 Thailand	7.8	10.0	8.9	7.5	7.8	7.9	7.8	7.7	7.7	7.6	7.5	7.4	7.8
33 Myammar	2.2	2.7	1.3	3.7	5.4	4.6	6.7	8.0	7.2	5.8	4.7	5.5	5.3
34 SEAO	3.7	2.6	2.5	3.7	7.4	8.1	8.1	8.2	9.2	8.7	8.3	7.9	7.2
35 Bangladesh	4.7	6.6	3.3	3.8	3.8	3.8	3.8	3.8	3.8	3.8	3.8	3.8	3.7
36 India	5.8	5.6	1.3	4.2	3.8	5.0	5.4	5.5	5.7	6.2	6.4	6.7	5.0
37 Pakistan	6.4	5.3	4.7	3.8	3.6	5.0	5.1	5.4	5.7	5.9	6.3	6.6	5.2
38 Sri Lanka	4.2	6.2	4.8	4.5	2.9	2.7	2.5	2.3	2.2	2.1	2.0	1.8	2.8
39 SWAO	3.8	5.2	4.8	2.7	2.6	3.1	3.1	3.1	3.1	3.1	3.1	3.1	3.2
40 Pacific Islands	1.6	.0	6.0	1.6	2.0	2.0	2.0	2.0	2.0	2.0	2.0	2.0	2.3
41 Iran,I.R.of	3.3	11.7	9.7	9.9	7.1	1.0	1.3	1.6	1.7	1.7	1.7	1.7	3.7
42 Iraq	6.0	4.3	-19.0	9.9	4.5	4.7	4.3	4.0	3.7	3.4	3.2	2.9	1.9
43 Israel	3.5	5.1	5.9	5.2	6.3	5.7	5.2	4.9	4.7	4.5	4.3	4.2	5.1
44 Kuwait	.1	5.2	-36.7	19.2	3.2	3.2	3.2	3.2	3.2	3.2	3.2	3.2	-.3
45 Saudi Arabia	-.6	2.5	2.5	2.3	4.7	5.5	5.4	5.2	5.2	5.1	5.0	5.0	4.6
46 MIDO	3.9	4.8	5.8	6.0	.7	5.5	4.0	4.1	4.0	4.1	4.2	4.2	4.2
47 Algeria	2.7	.0	.0	3.0	1.8	1.8	1.8	1.8	1.8	1.8	1.8	1.8	1.7

48 Egypt	4.9	2.6	2.3	2.8	2.7	2.7	2.8	2.8	2.8	2.9	2.9	2.9	2.7
49 Libya	-5.5	-2.6	-2.7	2.0	2.0	2.0	2.0	2.0	2.0	2.0	2.0	2.0	1.5
50 Morocco	3.8	3.7	5.1	1.0	3.3	3.1	3.0	3.0	3.0	3.1	3.1	3.1	3.1
51 Tunisia	3.7	7.6	3.9	-1.1	2.4	2.2	2.2	2.2	2.3	2.5	2.5	2.6	2.2
52 Ethiopia	2.0	-.4	-6.0	-5.5	-4.0	4.1	4.1	4.0	4.0	3.9	3.9	3.8	1.2
53 Gabon	.0	-2.4	-2.5	.7	.7	.7	.7	.7	.7	.7	.7	.7	.4
54 Ghana	2.2	3.3	4.2	2.7	3.0	.6	1.1	1.5	1.9	2.2	2.5	2.7	2.2
55 Kenya	4.2	5.2	4.9	2.0	3.1	3.1	3.1	3.1	3.2	3.2	3.2	3.2	3.2
56 Liberia	-1.2	-1.0	-1.0	6.4	1.0	.7	1.0	1.2	1.4	1.6	1.8	1.9	1.6
57 Nigeria	1.2	8.2	4.5	2.3	.9	.8	.9	1.1	1.3	1.4	1.5	1.5	1.6
58 Sudan	1.5	1.5	1.4	5.7	1.8	1.8	1.8	1.8	1.8	1.9	1.9	1.9	2.2
59 South Africa	1.7	2.2	2.2	-.7	2.2	1.8	1.7	1.7	1.6	1.6	1.6	1.5	1.5
60 SOSO	2.0	1.2	1.6	2.0	2.0	1.9	1.9	1.9	1.9	1.9	1.9	1.9	1.9
61 Argentina	-1.1	.1	8.9	8.5	4.6	1.7	1.5	1.5	1.7	2.1	2.2	2.3	3.5
62 Bolivia	.1	2.6	4.1	3.5	2.2	2.2	2.3	2.3	2.4	2.4	2.5	2.5	2.6
63 Brazil	1.5	-4.1	.9	-1.0	1.9	1.9	1.9	1.7	1.7	1.7	1.7	1.6	1.4
64 Chile	2.8	2.1	6.0	9.5	5.4	2.8	2.7	2.5	2.4	2.3	2.2	2.1	3.8
65 Colombia	3.5	4.1	2.3	2.7	2.6	2.5	2.1	1.6	1.8	2.1	2.1	2.0	2.2
66 Mexico	1.7	4.5	3.6	2.5	3.8	4.2	4.6	4.9	5.2	5.5	5.8	6.0	4.6
67 Ecuador	2.1	2.4	3.8	4.6	3.8	1.7	1.8	1.8	1.9	2.0	2.1	2.2	2.6
68 Paraguay	2.8	3.1	2.5	1.5	1.2	3.8	3.8	3.6	3.6	3.6	3.5	3.5	3.1
69 Peru	-.8	-4.4	2.7	-2.2	2.2	1.9	1.9	1.9	1.9	2.0	2.1	2.1	1.6
70 Uruguay	-.1	.9	2.9	5.5	.6	.7	.7	.7	.7	.8	.8	.8	1.4
71 Venezuela	.8	6.9	10.4	8.7	6.2	2.0	1.8	1.7	1.7	1.7	1.7	1.6	3.7
72 LACO	.1	1.4	2.7	1.8	2.7	2.8	3.0	3.1	3.2	3.3	3.4	3.4	2.9
73 Turkey	5.0	4.7	4.5	5.2	4.8	4.8	4.8	4.7	4.7	4.7	4.7	4.6	4.8
74 MEURO	1.9	1.7	1.6	-14.0	1.4	1.4	1.5	1.7	1.7	1.6	1.6	1.6	-.1
75 Bulgaria	1.8	-11.9	-11.8	-12.5	-7.3	-5.5	-1.8	3.8	3.4	3.1	2.9	2.6	-2.5
76 Czechoslovakia	1.0	-9.1	-16.7	-7.1	-1.9	.8	1.9	1.2	1.2	1.2	1.2	1.2	-1.9
77 Hungary	1.1	-3.3	-11.9	-5.9	.5	.7	2.7	3.0	2.8	2.6	2.5	2.3	-.2
78 Poland	-.1	-11.6	-7.6	.3	1.7	3.3	3.6	2.2	2.0	1.9	1.7	1.6	1.0
79 Romania	.8	-12.9	-13.6	-14.7	-3.5	1.8	1.6	1.3	1.5	1.6	1.7	1.7	-2.3
80 CIS (Former USSR)	2.0	-4.0	-8.0	-17.8	-12.8	-1.7	1.8	1.8	1.9	2.0	2.0	2.1	-3.1

THE QUARTERLY ECONOMETRIC MODELS OF THE POST-WAR JAPANESE ECONOMY AND THE RESONANCE EFFECT OF INTEREST RATE POLICY *

by

KEI MORI

Tokyo

Summary

The quarterly econometric models are estimated by the two-stage least squares method for the post-war Japanese economy from the 4th quarter of 1953 to 1st quarter of 1961. Some important parts of the public sector are treated as endogenous. Pseudo-realistic simulations are worked out for the studies on the growth rate and forecasts. By some experimental simulations it is suggested that there exists a resonance effect caused by interest rate policy. A built-in stabilizing effect is studied by calculating the various kinds of multipliers. The applicability tests with pseudo-realistic simulations are applied on the models used in the above studies.

1. Introduction

The post-war Japanese economy might be characterized by its rapid growth in comparison with that of foreign countries. The private sector has indeed contributed to this growth through its autonomous activity, but the role played by the public sector and its influence have been too

* This study is a sequel to the previous studies of author *K. Mori*, A Simulation Model of a Post-War Japanese Economy: 1953–1954. »Economic Studies Quarterly« (Rivonkeizaigaku) Vol. 13, NO. 3 (May 1963) pp. 45–67 (in Japanese). *K. Mori*. Simulation Analysis of the Cycles and Rapid Growth in the Japanese Economy (in Japanese). The Economic Growth in the Post-War Japanese Economy, edited by *Ryutaro Komiya* (October 1963), pp. 1912–20. The author is deeply indebted to professor Tadao Uchiad of Tokyo University for discussions at various stages of the studies. He wishes to express appreciation to Tokyo Center for Economic Research for grants. The work of putting this paper into English was financed by the Ford Foundation as part of a project for promoting the translation of Japanese economic studies.

great to be negligible. Therefore, the model, in which the public sector is treated as exogenous, seems to be unable to describe this rapid growth which is the joint effect of public and private activities. In order to explore this effect the author constructed the model which has an endogenous public sector as well as a private one. It is concisely named "*mixed model* or *model I*".

At the same time, for the convenience of comparison, the author formed the model, which has an endogenous private sector and an exogenous public sector, as a pair of the mixed model. It is shortly called "*private model* or *model II*". The term "pair" implies that each behavioristic equation in the private model is designed to include the same set of explanatory variables as those in the corresponding equation in the private sector of the mixed model.

The usual procedure for econometric model building consists of the following stages, i.e., "structure set-up (specifications)", "statistical estimations", and "statistical tests of hypotheses". Furthermore, the applicabilities test and dynamic properties test should be done, because any satisfactory econometric model is necessarily a multivariate autoregressive system, i.e., a simultaneous difference equation system, which contains lagged endogenous variables. If the result of these two kinds of tests mentioned above is feed back, the structure set-up will be more effectively improved. The economic model building itself will, accordingly, constitute "a feed back system "accompanied with trial and error.

Models I and II, shown in the appendix, are constructed through the process of such repeated tests, keeping the consistent relations between the structure set-up and the tests. Without the applicabilities tests, it might hardly be known how much the structural equation has contributed to the applicability of the model and whether or not any modification has caused the expected improvement.

The basic strategy adopted here is the "priority improvement" of the structural equations. The priority improvement means as follows. First, structural equations of the model are separated into the following two groups. One is the group of structural equations which have passed two tests mentioned above. These equations have specifications on which the majority of researchers will agree. The other is the group of structural equations which have turned out to have gross defects by the results of these tests. The former group being not modified, the latter group would be rather steadily improved. In other words, the "priority improvement" strategy might be expected to bring each structural equation in the model to have the balanced power of explanation. The important equations of the latter group, in our case, are the structural equations regarding private inventory investment and private investment of producers' durable equipment etc., which have been regarded as the weak points of macro econometric models.

The final form of the model, which is on the basis of quarterly national income data will be of a type giving priority to behavioristic equations concerning to expenditures complemented with those on distributed shares. These models are estimated by the two stage least squares method, using the set of all the predetermined variables, not separated block-wise.

The models are constructed on thirty quarterly observations from the fourth quarter of 1953 to the first quarter of 1961. The estimated structural equations are presented in appendix (A–2), with the variables and the sources of data listed in appendix (A–1). In section 2 the models and their individual equations are described.

Simulations are made in this study to these quarterly econometric models to some analyses of pseudo-realistic situations, growth rates, forecasts, effects of interest rate policy and a built-in stabilizing effect.

Whenever there had existed a sharp decline in the difference of the current value of GNP from its value of the same quarter in the preceding year, a policy to raise official interest rate, i.e., tight money policy, had been adopted by the monetary authority. With respect to these facts, there are alternative two points of view. The one insists that the decline in the difference of GNP was exogenously caused by the change of the official interest rate. The other argued that these are resulted from endogenous movements generated by systematic parts of the economic mechanism rather than results of interest rate policies.

In section 4. the author will suggest a somewhat different interpretation that there has existed the resonance phenomenon caused by the interaction between the interest rate policy and the inherent oscillation of our economic system.

In order to test the applicability of our models, pseudo-realistic simulations run from the fourth quarter of 1954 to the first quarter of 1961. And, the extrapolative simulations run from the fourth quarter of 1954 to the first quarter of 1965 in order to forecast the magnitudes of the major components of GNP on the expenditures and distributive shares. Section 3 describes the results of these pseudo-realistic simulations. Section 5 contains the studies on the various multipliers of the fiscal policies and a built-in stabilizing effect.

2. *Assumptions in the Structure of the Model*

The individual structural equations incorporated in the model will be described in the below. Almost each estimated coefficient satisfies the sign condition imposed on the structural coefficient, except for a few cases in which some remarks will be given. Almost all the variables are the real valued ones evaluated in constant price of 1955 calendar year. As a result, for instance, various tax functions are expressed in real terms instead of nominal ones. Obviously this may be a defect of our model, but we can suppose that it is considerably weakened by including the real valued variables deflating by the same price index on both sides of these tax functions. This approach provides us with a great advantage of operating the model without the difficulties caused by nonlinearities.

It is assumed in the *private consumption function* that the consumers' expenditure C_t depends upon the current disposable income Y_{dt} and the maximum among the four quarters moving averages of past consumptions $\underset{\tau \leq t}{Max}\ (\overset{4}{\underset{s=1}{Av}}\ (C_{t-s}))$. The subscript t refers to the time point or period at which the variable in question (stock or flow, respectively, as the case may be) is measured. Let Q_{it} be the dummy variable of the seasonal shift ($i = 2, 3, 4$). If *t–th* period corresponds to *i–th* quarter, then Q_{it} is unity, otherwise, Q_{it} is zero for all t. Let u_{gt} be the random disturbances in the *g–th* equation. The *private consumption function* may be written in the form

$$C_t = a_0 + a_1 Y_{dt} + a_2 Max\ (Av\ (C_{t-s})) + a_3 Q_{2t} + a_4 Q_{3t} + a_5 Q_{4t} + u_{1t} \tag{2.1}$$

The parameter to be estimated from the sample data is denoted by lower case Latin character.

We shall specify that successive disturbances u_{gt} are independent of each other, and further that their distribution is the same for all time periods. The joint distribution of the components u_{gt} of the vector u_t is specified to be normal, with the following parameters:

$$E(u_{gt}) = O,\ E(u_{gt}u_{ht}) = \sigma_{gh} > O\ (g, h = 1, 2. \ldots, G)$$

where the symbol E is an operator denoting that the expected value is to be taken of the random variable.

The *gross private residential housing construction function* assumes that the residential construction I_{Ht} depends upon the current disposable income Y_{dt} and the loanable funds with two periods lag L_{Ht-2}, which is supplied by the government at low rate of interest in aiding constructing of personal residential housing. This function may be written as follows:

$$I_{Ht} = b_0 + b_1 Ydt + b_2 L_{Ht-2} + b_3 Q_{2t} + b_4 Q_{3t} + b_5 Q_{4t} + u_{2t} \tag{2.2}$$

The assumption here implies that personal housing construction is mainly restricted by the personal capabilities to procure funds because of an existing, unsaturated, large potential excess demand for residential housing, and that the change of population may have an influence not on the realized demand but on the potential demand.

The *gross private investment in producers' durable equipment function* assumes that the gross private fixed investment I_{Ft} depends upon the current corporate profit after tax $(PC - TC)_t$, the stock of capital in the form of producers' durable equipment at the end of the preceding period K_{Ft-1}, and the three periods lagged value of the corporate profit after tax $(P_c - T_c)_{t-3}$. Therefore, the function may be written in the form:

$$I_{Ft} = c_0 + c_1\ (P_C - T_C) + c_2 K_{Ft-1} + c_3\ (P_C - T_C)_{t-3} + c_4 Q_{2t} + c_5 Q_{3t} + c_6 Q_{4t} + u_{3t} \tag{2.3}$$

This assumption implies that entrepreneur invests according the profit principle.

It should, however, be noted that investment depends upon the preceding stock of capital equipment significantly and that the sign of the estimate of c_2 has not been negative but positive. If we may assume that there exist the distributed lags between net investment and other explanatory variables and, at the same time, that the depreciation function for fixed capital stock (as is shown below) gives the rate of depreciation in the stationary state, then the estimate of c_2 may be considered to include the positive effects caused by these factors[1]. Therefore, if the value of the estimate minus the sum of these effects is negative, the net effect of the preceding capital stock on investment may be negative in spite of positive estimate c_2.

The *import function* assumes that the import M_t depends upon the private gross investment in producers' durable equipment I_{Ft}, the private inventory investment J_t and the average agreed rate of interest on loans and discounts i_{t-1}. This assumption implies that the main part of imported goods consists of producers' durable equipment and raw material which are required for domestic productions, and it is restricted by financial conditions. It may be written in the form;

$$M_t = d_0 + d_1 I_{Ft} + d_2 J_t + d_3 i_{t-1} + d_4 Q_{2t} + d_5 Q_{3t} + d_6 Q_{4t} + u_{4t} \tag{2.4}$$

The *export function* assumes that the export E_t depends upon the index of transacted quantities in world trade M_{Wt} and the preceding capital stock in the form of producers' durable equipment K_{Ft-1}. The preceding capital stock is adopted to represent a states of capacity and quality of technology in production of export goods. It may be written in the form:

$$E_t = e_0 + e_1 M_{Wt} + e_2 K_{Ft-1} + e_3 Q_{2t} + e_4 Q_{3t} + e_5 Q_{4t} + u_{5t} \tag{2.5}$$

Private inventory investment J_t is calculated from the following identity by using *private inventory stock function:*

$$J_t = K_{Jt} - K_{Jt-1}$$

The *private inventory stock function* assumes that the private inventory stock K_{Jt} depends upon the average private gross national income over the preceding one year $\underset{s=1}{\overset{4}{Av}}\,(GNP^*_{t-s})$, the preceding outstanding order received for machinery O_{t-1} and the preceding average agreed rate of interest on loans and discounts i_{t-1}. This implies that the inventory stock is mainly determined as the desired level which corresponds to the general activity level of production in the private sector, and it is restricted by financial conditions. This function may be written in the form:

[1] See *R. C. Liu,* An Exploratory Quarterly Econometric Model of Effective Demand in the Postwar U.S. Economy. "Econometrica", Vol. 31 (1963), p. 305, footnote 7.

$$K_{Jt} = f_0 + f_1 \overset{4}{\underset{s=1}{Av}} (GNP^*_{t-s}) + f_2 O_{t-1} + f_3 i_{t-1} + f_4 Q_{2t} + f_5 Q_{3t} + f_6 Q_{4t} + u_{6t} \quad (2.6)$$

Two capital consumption allowance (depreciation) functions are described as follow. The first one is the *private residential capital consumption allowance function* and the second one is the *private capital consumption allowance on producers' durable equipment function.* It is assumed in the former that the residential capital consumption allowance D_{Ht} depends upon the disposable income Y_{dt} and the average value of current and preceding stock of capital in the form of residential houses $(K_{Ht} + K_{Ht-1})/2$. In the latter it is assumed that the capital consumption allowances on producers' durable equipment D_{Ft} depends upon only the average value of current and preceding stock of capital in the form of producers' durable equipment $(K_{Ft} + K_{Ft-1})/2$.

$$D_{Ht} = g_0 + g_1 Y_{dt} + g_2 (K_{Ht} + K_{Ht-1})/2 + g_3 Q_{2t} + g_4 Q_{3t} + g_5 Q_{4t} + u_{7t} \quad (2.7)$$

$$D_{Ft} = h_0 + h_1 (K_{Ft} + K_{Ft-1})/2 + h_2 Q_{2t} + h_3 Q_{3t} + h_4 Q_{4t} + u_{8t} \quad (2.8)$$

These functions are formulated upon the basis of *Klein-Goldberger*'s discussion of the depreciation function and slightly modified through the results of several statistical tests. The same procedures as mentioned above are adopted in some other functions, e.g., the distributive shares functions. All these forms of specifications have already been tested by the author (8). These modified *Klein-Goldberger* formulations are shown as follows:

$$W_t = i_0 + i_1 GNP^*_t + i_2 Q_{2t} + i_3 Q_{3t} + i_4 Q_{4t} + u_{9t} \quad (2.9)$$

$$A_t = j_0 + j_1 GNP^*_t + j_2 Q_{2t} + j_3 Q_{3t} + j_4 Q_{4t} + u_{10t} \quad (2.10)$$

$$P_{ct} = k_0 + k_1 P_t + k_2 P_{ct-1} + u_{11t} \quad (2.11)$$

$$S_{ct} = l_0 + l_1 (P_{ct} - T_{ct}) + l_2 (P_{ct-1} - T_{ct-1} - S_{ct-1}) + l_3 i_{t-1} + u_{12t} \quad (2.12)$$

W_t = Compensation of employees
A_t = Proprietors' income
P_{ct} = Corporate income
T_{ct} = Corporate tax
GNP^*_t = Gross national private income
S_{ct} = Retained corporate profit increment
i_{t-1} = Preceding average agreed rate of interest on loans and discounts

The *public expenditures functions* are concerning *consumption expenditure* and *inventory investment* which are not regarded as the means of governmental policies but as the variables determined by the activity levels of government and national economy. Therefore, only the governmental investment in durable equipment is regarded as the means of governmental policy, i.e., the exogenous variable in our mixed model. Of course all functions, which will be described below, do not belong to the private model but only the mixed model. These public expenditures functions may be written in the forms:

$$G_{ct} = m_0 + m_1 GNP_t + m_2 Q_{2t} + m_3 Q_{3t} + m_4 Q_{4t} + u_{13t} \quad (2.13)$$

$$G_{Jt} = n_0 + n_1 G_t + n_2 \Delta G_t + n_3 Q_{2t} + n_4 Q_{3t} + n_5 Q_{4t} + u_{14t} \quad (2.14)$$

G_{ct} = Government consumption

G_t = Government purchases of goods and services

G_{Jt} = Government inventory investment

GNP_t = Gross national product

$\Delta G_t = G_t - G_{t-1}$

The *contribution by the government to social insurance* H_t, which is fifty percent of the total, is assumed to depend upon the gross private national income GNP^*_t and time t.

$$H_t = o_0 + o_1 GNP^*_t + o_2 t + o_3 Q_{2t} + o_4 Q_{3t} + o_5 Q_{4t} + u_{15t} \quad (2.15)$$

Three tax functions are formulated in the terms of real value as is described at the beginning of this section. The *indirect enterprise tax function* assumes that the net indirect tax T^*_t depends upon gross national product GNP_t and time t.

$$T^*_t = p_0 + p_1 GNP_t + p_2 t + p_3 Q_{2t} + p_4 Q_{3t} + p_5 Q_{4t} + u_{16t} \quad (2.16)$$

The indirect tax which has been steadily increasing its weight in the whole tax revenues is now the stable source of governmental revenues. The *personal income tax function* assumes that personal income tax T_{pt} depends upon two taxable incomes which are a compensation of employees W_t and proprietors' income A_t.

$$T_{pt} = q_0 + q_2 W_t' + q_3 A_t + q_4 Q_{2t} + q_5 Q_{3t} + q_6 Q_{4t} + u_{17t} \quad (2.17)$$

Corporate tax function assumes that corporate tax T_{ct} depends upon the preceding corporate income P_{ct-1}.

$$T_{ct} = r_0 + r_1 P_{ct-1} + r_2 Q_{2t} + r_3 Q_{3t} + r_4 Q_{4t} + u_{18t} \quad (2.18)$$

The specification for this function to include the current corporate income P_{ct} is rejected by t-test on the coefficient. The one period lag is naturally explained by institutional time lag in collecting the tax.

The identities in our models are shown in Appendix A — 2 (ii).

3. *Pseudo-Realistic Simulations*

All ten simulations concerning the models mentioned in the previous section started from the fourth quarter of 1954 as the initial period. Their respective features are to be referred to at the beginning of each paragraph, as they are required. In this section, the pseudo-realistic situations of Japanese economy are analyzed through the final test and the computation of its endogenous growth rate, by using three simulations.

In general, "simulation" means the systematic operation of such a simple model that is efficiently abstracted from the mechanism controlling a real world for the purpose of analoginizing the behaviors of the model to the real ones or to the ones which will possibly happen and clarifying the various properties of a real world. Hence the simulation turns out to be meaningful, if and only if the model satisfies the following two conditions.

The first condition is that various characteristics of the real mechanism should sufficiently be reflected in the model. The second is that is should be possible to operate the model with a greater ease than the real mechanism.

Two conditions mentioned above are examined for our model. The first is whether or not the model is valid, and the second is whether or not the model can be easily solved in each experimental simulation. There is no problem in the latter because ten simulations have actually been solved. On the other hand, there will be no complete methodology to confirm the validity of model. Therefore the following two kinds of tests are tentatively made. One is the statistical test, and the other is the test concerning the applicability of its dynamic solution. The main contents of the first test are the F-test on the residuals through the multiple correlation coefficient, the t-test on the ratio of its standard deviation to the value of estimated coefficient and the *von Neumann* ratio test of non serial correlation on the residuals, which are usually used. The second one is to test whether or not the extent of discrepancy between the theoretical value and the actual value on the time series of endogenous variables included in the model is recognizable. The reduced form derived from the mixted model is used for this test[1]. In the following the reduced form of the mixed model is denoted by π_I, and that of private model, π_{II}.

i) Pseudo-realistic situation

The three simulations presented in this section are made on the mixed model in Appendix (A) in the following manner. Let y_t be G dimensional vector of the current values of the jointly endogenous variables. Z_t is the K_1 dimensional vector of the predetermined endogenous variables[2]. Let x_t be the K_2 dimensional vector of exogenous variables. Let A, B and C be respectively $G \times G$, $G \times K_1$ and $G \times K_2$ matrices of the structural coefficients of appropriate orders. The model may be written in the form

$$Ay_t = Bz_t + Cx_t \tag{1}$$

[1] This kind of test on the private model is also made.

[2] $Z_t = Z\,(y_{t-1}, \ldots\ldots\ldots\ldots, y_{t-t^{\circ}})$

Z_t is the function of $y_{t-1}, \ldots\ldots\ldots\ldots, y_{t-t^{\circ}}$, and function Z is not always linear, where t° is the maximum lag in the model, because nonlinear term, Max $\{Av(c)\}$ is a component of vector Z_t.

or if A is a nonsingular matrix

$$y_t = A^{-1}Bz_t + A^{-1}Cx_t \tag{2}$$

where A^{-1} is the inverse of matrix A. The expression (2) is the reduced form of (1).

There are two types of solutions, i.e., a final solution and a total solution, named by *Goldberger* for the reduced form (2).

The final solution is obtained by substituting the theoretical value for the predetermined endogenous variable Z_t in each iteration, with exception of the first iteration where the actual value is substituted. Therefore, this is the true solution of the difference equation system.

On the contrary, total solution is the one which is obtained by applying the same procedure in every iteration as in the initial iteration. That is to say, the actual value is substituted for z_t in every iteration. By the way, the actual value is substituted for x_t in every iteration in case of obtaining both types of solutions. The *pseudo-realistic situation* means the final solution in the above-mentioned situation. This total solution may be written in the following simplified form:

$$y^T{}_t = \pi_I (\bar{x}_t, \bar{z}_t) \tag{3}$$

where the bar on the variables in the parenthesis indicates that the actual value is substituted for them, and y^T is defined as a function of outside information.

As *simulation I*, the final solution in this situation may be written as follows.

$$y^F{}_t = \pi_I (\bar{x}_t \mid \bar{z}_{1954:4}) \tag{4}$$

where vector $\bar{z}_{1954:4}$ is the set of the actual values of predetermined endogenous variables in the fourth quarter of 1954, which is given as the initial value.

It may be necessary to examine the correlation coefficient between the theoretical value and actual value of the sequences of thirty endogenous variables from the fourth quarter of 1954 to the first quarter of 1961.

See the first two columns in Table 3.1.

Let the correlation coefficient of final solution to the actual value be R_F, and similarly the correlation coefficient of total solution to the actual value, R_T. Now, $(1 - R_F) \,/\, (1 - R_T)$ is calculated on each variable. This shows the ratio between the part remains unexplained by the final solution in the movement of actual value and the part remains unexplained by the total solution in the movement of actual value. Roughly speaking, this shows that the higher the ratio in a certain endogenous variable is, the more dynamically the influence of all the estimated disturbances before this period is amplified[1].

---

[1] As a result, it corresponds to the ratio of residual standard deviations. A strict discussion has not been fully entered into, but it may be written as follows by denoting the actual value in $t-th$ period by $\bar{y}_t$, final solution, $y^F{}_t$ and total solution, $y^T{}_t$;

Table 3.1

Correlation Coefficients between Actual and Simulated Values

	Simulation I: $\pi_I(\bar{x}_t \mid \bar{z}_{1954:4})$			Simulation II: $\pi_I(\bar{O}_{t-1}, \bar{i}_{t-1}, \hat{x}^o_t \mid \bar{z}_{1954:4})$	
	R_F	$\dfrac{(1-R_F)}{(1-R_T)}$	R_T	R_F	R_T
GNP	0.958	1.40	0.970	0.965	0.980
C	0.976	1.60	0.985	0.980	0.988
G_C	0.973	1.04	0.974	0.973	0.975
I_F	0.927	5.21	0.986	0.977	0.986
J	0.604	2.44	0.838	0.675	0.838
G_J	0.703	1.27	0.766	0.809	0.820
W	0.935	1.55	0.958	0.947	0.954
A	0.986	0.74	0.981	0.984	0.981
P_C	0.829	1.45	0.882	0.902	0.889
S_C	0.490	2.79	0.817	0.546	0.838
H	0.973	1.23	0.978	0.962	0.967
T_C	0.870	4.81	0.973	0.921	0.973
T_v	0.926	0.96	0.923	0.922	0.913
T^*	0.964	1.29	0.972	0.962	0.968
E	0.983	1.00	0.983	0.969	0.970
M	0.932	2.17	0.969	0.968	0.970
D_H	0.984	1.27	0.959	0.961	0.973
D_F	0.991	1.13	0.992	0.992	0.991
K_J	0.991	2.50	0.996	0.980	0.996

As a result, 5.2 of private investment for fixed equipment (I_F) and 4.8 of corporate tax (T_C) are extremely high, and 2.8 of undistributed corporate profits (S_C), 2.4 of private inventory investment (J) and 2.2 of import follow next. For GNP, it is 1.4. However, for the following items it is larger than GNP; i.e., 1.6 for the private consumption expenditure (C), 1.5 for the compensation of employees (W) and Government contribution to social security (H) and 1.5 for the corporate profits (P_C). On the other hand, for the following it is, 1.0 or less than 1.0, i.e., 1.0 for the export (E) and Government expenditure (G_C), 0.9 for the personal income tax (T_p) and 0.7 for the proprietor's income (A).

ii) Forecasts and Growth Rate Analysis

In regard to nine exogenous variables included in this model, the actual value is substituted for the outstanding orders received for

$$\bar{y}_t = Tu_t \cdot Tu_{t-1} \cdot \cdots\cdots\cdots\cdots Tu_1 \cdot \bar{z}$$
$$y^F_t = T \cdot T \cdot \cdots\cdots\cdots\cdots T \cdot \bar{z}$$
$$y^T_t = T \cdot Tu_{t-1} \cdot \cdots\cdots\cdots\cdots Tu_1 \cdot \bar{z}$$

T is the iterative operator including x_t, and Tu_t includes the residual in addition to it.

machinery of the previous period O_{t-1} and the averages of agreed interest rates on loans and discounts of the previous period i_{t-1}[1], and the computed values of extrapolation equation are substituted for all other exogenous variables $\hat{x}^o_t$ excluding dummy variables showing the seasonal shift Q_{it} and time variable t. This may be written as;

$$(5) \qquad y^F_t = \pi_I (\bar{O}_{t-1}, \bar{i}_{t-1}, \hat{x}^o_t \mid \bar{z}_{1954:4})$$

Simulation II.

If the computed value[2] of extrapolation equation $\hat{x}_t$ is substituted for every exogenous variable, the equation may be written as;

$$(6) \qquad y^F_t = \pi_I (\hat{x}_t \mid \bar{z}_{1954:4})$$

Simulation III.

Simulation III should naturally be used for the forecast, but actually simulation II is used for the forecasting for the following reasons, and simulation III is used for examining the dynamic properties of the model.

The first reason is that both O_{t-1} and i_{t-1} have notable cyclical parts other than seasonal shifts and cannot be represented by a simple trend factor.

The second is that they are available more than one year earlier than all other exogenous variables. Therefore, there is an advantage of increasing the forecasting power between the end of observation period and the period proceeding the present one.

For these reasons, the forecasting was made with the simulation II utilizing the information concerning cyclical fluctuations of i_{t-1}, O_{t-1}.

It can be said, from Table 3.1, that Simulation II is excellent judging from the highly precise forecast of Simulation II in comparison with Simulation I (pseudo-realistic situation).

The time path of the dynamic solution of Simulation III, which includes only the *time trend,* excluding the part of cyclical fluctuations of O_{t-1}, i_{t-1} is also examined.

The solution for the intrinsic growth rate of the model is partly shown in Fig. 3.2 through Simulation III. But the growth rate obtained here is in terms of the difference of the current values from those of the same

[1] The actual value is substituted from the second quarter of 1961 to the first quarter of 1962, and conjectured values is substituted for later periods.

[2] Extrapolation equation is given in the following form.

$$\hat{x}_t = L_0 + L_1 t + L_2 Q_{2t} + L_3 Q_{3t} + L_4 Q_{4t}$$

t is 1 for the first quarter of 1952. Each estimated equation is shown in Appendix A — 2 (iii).

$$\left.\begin{matrix}\text{the rate of}\\ \text{growth}\end{matrix}\right\} = \frac{GNP_t - GNP_{t-4}}{GNP_{t-4}} = \left\{\frac{GNP_t}{GNP_{t-4}}\right\} - 1 = \left\{\begin{matrix}\text{ratio of current}\\ \text{value to that of}\\ \text{the same quarter}\\ \text{in the proceeding}\\ \text{year.}\end{matrix}\right\} - 1.$$

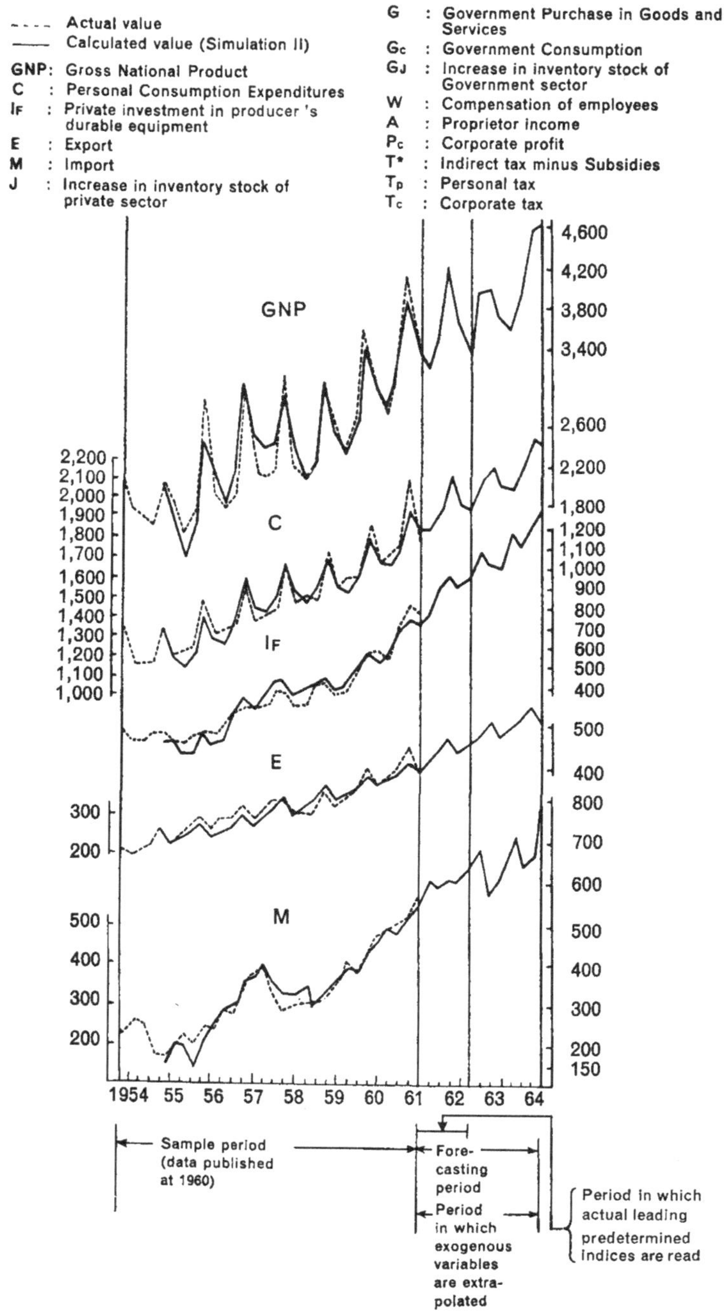

---- Actual value
—— Calculated value (Simulation II)
GNP: Gross National Product
C : Personal Consumption Expenditures
IF : Private investment in producer 's durable equipment
E : Export
M : Import
J : Increase in inventory stock of private sector
G : Government Purchase in Goods and Services
Gc : Government Consumption
GJ : Increase in inventory stock of Government sector
W : Compensation of employees
A : Proprietor income
Pc : Corporate profit
T* : Indirect tax minus Subsidies
Tp : Personal tax
Tc : Corporate tax
GNP
C
IF
E
M
1954 55 56 57 58 59 60 61 62 63 64
Sample period (data published at 1960)
Fore-casting period
Period in which exogenous variables are extra-polated
Period in which actual leading predetermined indices are read

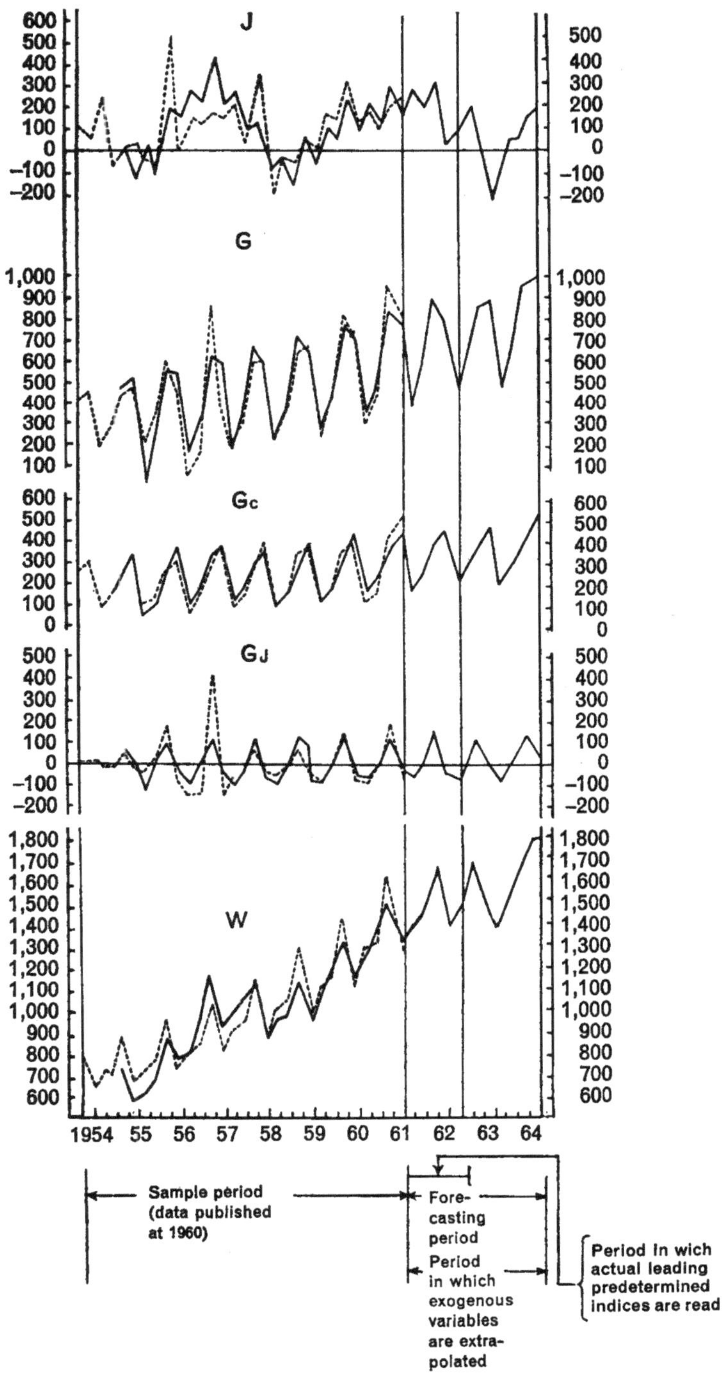
J
G
Gc
GJ
W
1954 55 56 57 58 59 60 61 62 63 64
Sample period (data published at 1960)
Forecasting period
Period in which exogenous variables are extrapolated
Period in wich actual leading predetermined indices are read

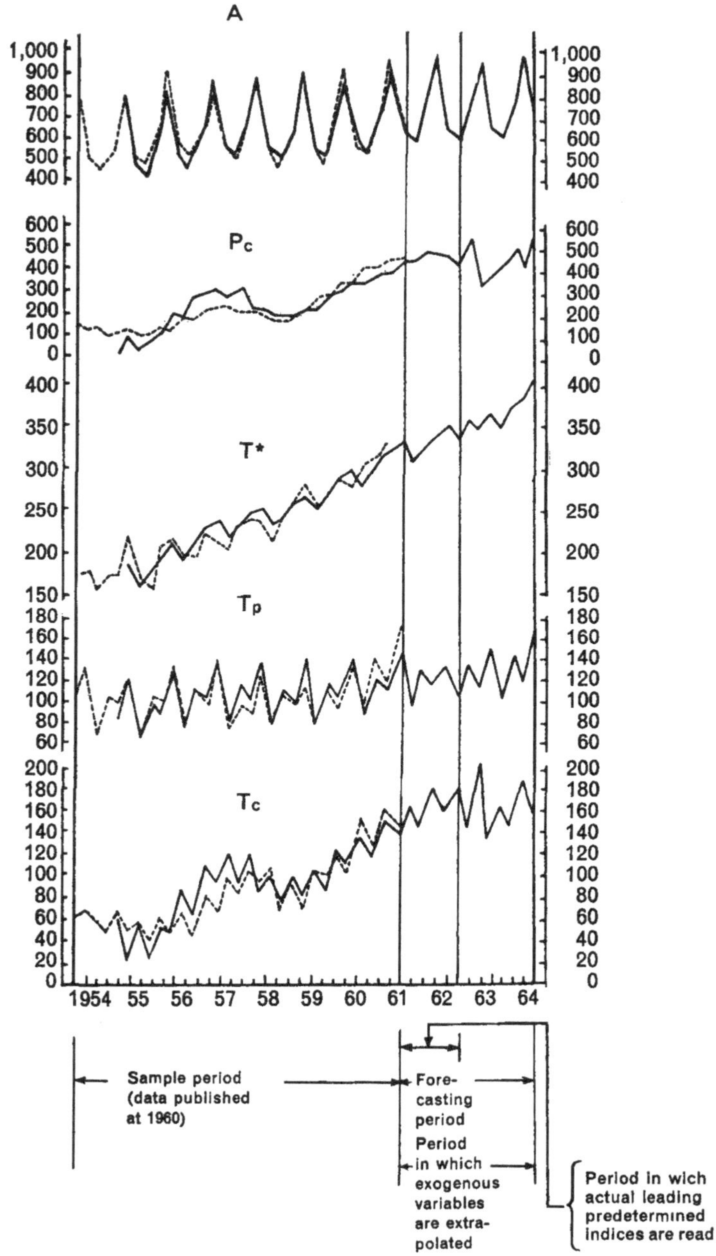

Fig. 3.1
Simulation Using by Model Estimated Two-stage Least Squares

Fig. 3.2 *Growth Rate of GNP*

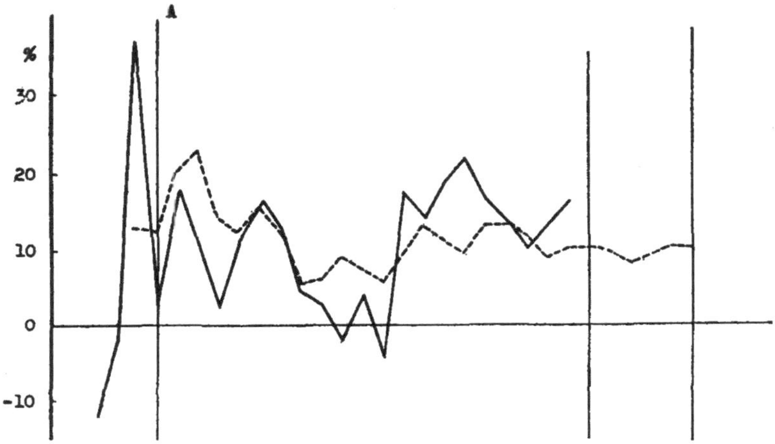

Actual growth rate of *GNP*

Growth rate of *GNP* by Simulation III

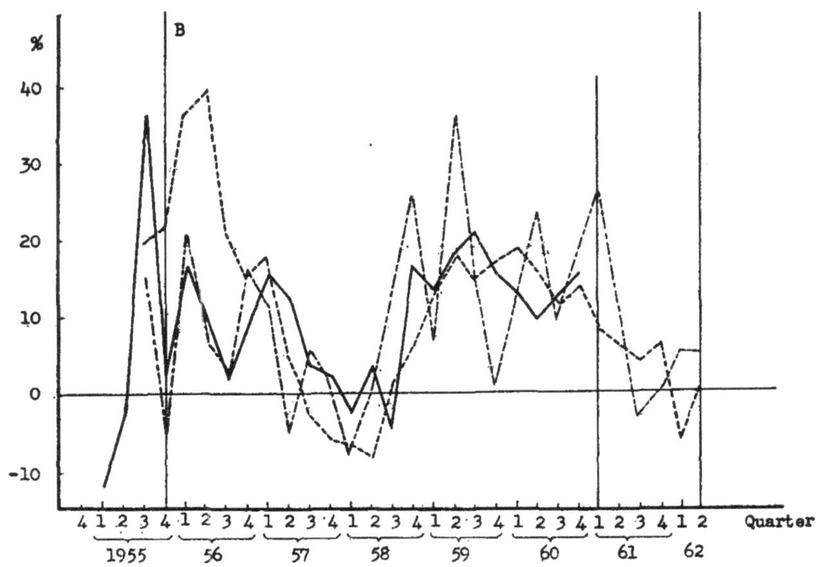

Actual growth rate of *GNP*

Growth rate of *GNP* by Simulation I

Growth rate of *GNP* by Simulation II

quarter in the preceding year. In this figure, the theoretical values of growth rate which obtain in Simulation I and II, in addition to Simulation III, are shown. This shows that the growth rate of an average of 10% is maintained excluding the two periods from the latter half of 1957 to 1958 and from the latter half of 1961 to 1962.

This shows that the growth rate of nearly 10% can be kept if all the exogenous variables continue to grow with the trend so far. It should be noted, however, that the influence on the growth rate exerted by the fluctuations of O_{t-1}, i_{t-1} is by no means small.

The annual values of the forecast and the annual growth rates obtained by Simulation II is shown in Table 3.2. This is shown in terms of real value evaluated using the prices of 1955. But this annual value is calculated in the fiscal year.

Then the forecasting power of this model is examined by comparing the forecasting values of 1961 with the actual value. Needless to say, the actual values of 1961 could not be used in the estimation of models.

The results are shown in Table 3.2. Generally speaking, each term of the expenditure enjoys a good forecast both in the annual value and in the annual growth rate. Better results are obtained than was expected for the private inventory investment (J)[1] and the private fixed invest-

Table 3.2
Actual Value & Calculated Value of 1961 Fiscal Year Growth Rate
(Unit of Amount: a billion yen)

	Actual Value	Calculated Value
GNP (Gross National Product)	15,214.0 (14.6%)	14,629.6 (11.3%)[a]
C (Private Consumption Expenditure)	7,763.4 (8.7%)	7,696.6 (8.8%)
I_F (Private Investment in Producer's Durable Equipment)	3,685.5 (26.9%)	3,618.1 (27.9%)
J (Increase in Inventory Stock of Private Sector)	1,158.4 (44.9%)	1,235.5 (45.6%)
E (Export)	1,821.5 (7.3%)	1,815.0 (9.2%)
M (Import)	2,590.8 (23.5%)	2,406.2 (18.7%)
G (Gross Government Purchase)	2,967.0 (18.3%)	2,668.9 (9.1%)

[a] The calculated value of *GNP* obtained by substituting actual values for G_F (Government investment in fixed assets) is 15,277.8 (16.3%) which is closer to the actual value.

[1] There have been few multiple correlation coefficients of inventory investment functions which exceed 0.6. When this function is built-in as a structural equation in the model, the applicability of the whole final solution of the model is in many cases, violated. See *K. Mori*, "Simulation Experiment for Japanese Economy 1953–1957, Information Processing in Japan", Vol. I (1961), pp. 79–94 and *T. Uchida* and *K. Mori*, "Simulation Analysis of Japanese Economy" (in Japanese) Atarashii Keizaibunseki (New Economic Analysis) edited by *M. Morishima*, *M. Shinohara* and *T. Uchida*, September 1960, pp. 211–242, Sobunsha Co., Tokyo.

ment (I_F), the precision of which have not been well forecast by the econometric models. For example, J shows the overestimation of only less than 1% in the high growth rate of 45%. And for I_F, the error is only 1% for the growth rate of 27%. The private consumption expenditure (C) shows the overestimation of 0.1% for the growth rate a little less than 9%, but it is underestimated in the annual level. The export is properly estimated, but for the import, the rapid increase of 1961 is not well forecast.

GNP is underestimated nearly 3% for the actual growth rate of 14%. This is considered to be mainly due to the underestimation of nearly 9% of the Government purchase of goods and services (G). The extrapolated value of the Government investment for fixed equipment occupying a considerably great weight in G may result from the underestimation of the rapid increase of the actual value in 1961.

4. *Resonance Effects of Fluctuating Interest Rate Policies*

i) Business Cycle Analysis

The recession occurred only once in the period from 1955 to 1960. Since the object of the following analysis is restricted to this only one phenomenon, the result of the analysis can not always be generalized. A kind of speculation may however be made as to the recession which occurred in the latter half of 1961 since the model used for the simulations embodies the dynamic properties of the business cycles in accordance with the structure of the Japanese economy. It is difficult to observe the obvious features of the business cycle as far as the absolute level of the variables are concerned since the Japanese economy is enjoying a strong upward trend. Therefore, "the difference of the current value of *GNP* from its value of the same quarter in the preceding year" (hereinafter called the difference) is analysed as the index of fluctuation of the growth rate. The fluctuation of the difference of the actual value of *GNP* is shown with a thick solid line in Fig. 4.1. The reduced form derived from the structure, i.e., Equation (2) is rewritten as follows:

(7) $$y_t = A^{-1}Bz_t + A^{-1}Cx_t = P_1 z_t + P_2 x_t$$

where

(8) $$P_1 = A^{-1}B, P_2 = A^{-1}C$$

Let the difference of y_t to be denoted Dy_t, the equation becomes as follows:

(9) $$\begin{aligned} Dy_t = y_t - y_{t-4} &= P_1 (z_t - z_{t-4}) + P_2 (x_t - x_{t-4}) \\ &= P_1 Dz_t + P_2 Dx_t \end{aligned}$$

The same relation as Equation (7) is obtained in the terms of Dy_t, Dz_t and Dx_t. The second term of the right hand side in Equation (9) is written in detail as follows:

(10) $$P_2 Dx_t = P_{21} (x_{1t} - x_{1,\, t-4}) + \cdots\cdots + P_{2k_2} (x_{k_2 t} - x_{k_2,\, t-4})$$

Fig. 4.1 *Difference of GNP: Actual Value and Simulation I & II*

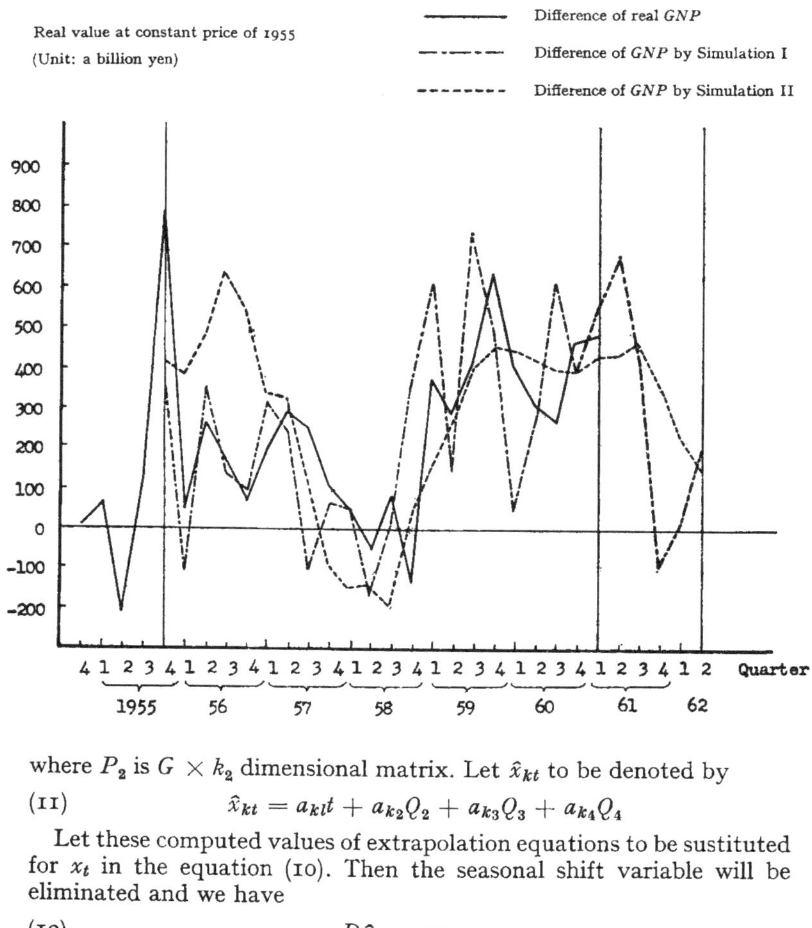

where P_2 is $G \times k_2$ dimensional matrix. Let $\hat{x}_{kt}$ to be denoted by

$$\hat{x}_{kt} = a_{kl}t + a_{k2}Q_2 + a_{k3}Q_3 + a_{k4}Q_4 \tag{11}$$

Let these computed values of extrapolation equations to be sustituted for x_t in the equation (10). Then the seasonal shift variable will be eliminated and we have

$$D\hat{x}_t = 4a_1 \tag{12}$$

Therefore, (10) becomes $P_2Dx_t = 4P_2a_1$.

Evidently, the direct contribution of the difference of the computed value of extrapolation equation to Dy_t is the constant value independent of the time. It depends only on the coefficient of the time variable in the respective extrapolation equation.

Therefore, the time path of the difference of simulation III is the intrinsic dynamic path of the model generated endogenously in case that $\hat{x}_t$ is substituted for exogenous variables. This may be clarified with Fig. 3.2 obtained from the above mentioned growth rate analysis, and the behavior of the difference is shown with a thick solid line in

Fig. 4.2. This is the moderate damping oscillation. The period of the oscillation is observed to be about three years.

Fig. 4.2 *Difference of GNP: Simulation III, IV, & V*

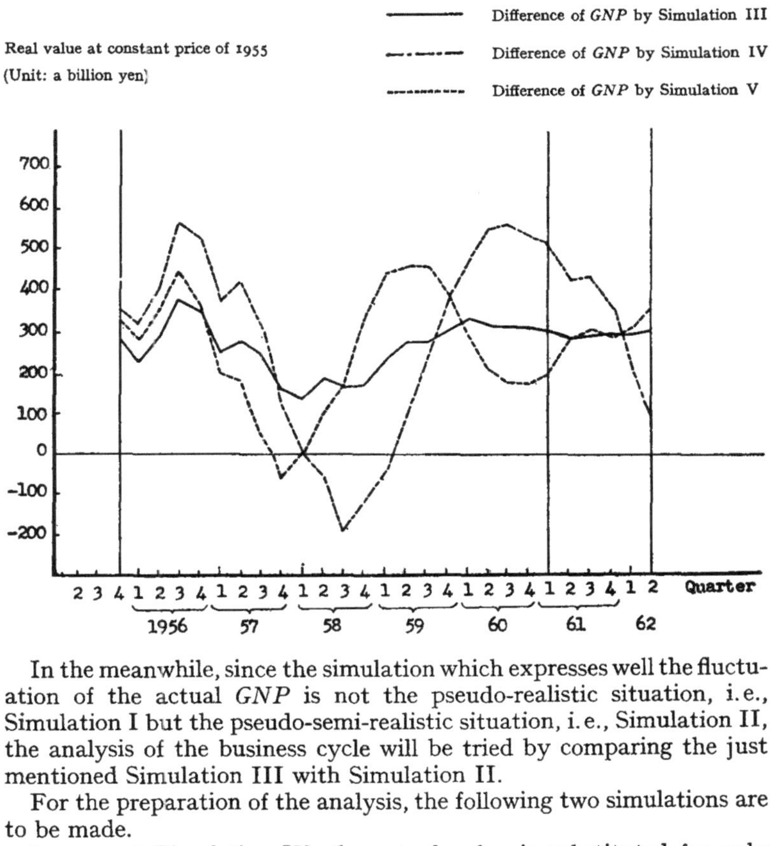

In the meanwhile, since the simulation which expresses well the fluctuation of the actual *GNP* is not the pseudo-realistic situation, i.e., Simulation I but the pseudo-semi-realistic situation, i.e., Simulation II, the analysis of the business cycle will be tried by comparing the just mentioned Simulation III with Simulation II.

For the preparation of the analysis, the following two simulations are to be made.

In case of *Simulation IV*, the actual value is substituted for only O_{t-1} and the computed value of the extrapolation equation for other exogenous variables.

$$y^F_t = \pi_I (\bar{O}_{t-1}, \hat{x}^o_t \mid \bar{z}_{1954:4}) \tag{13}$$

In case of *Simulation V*, the actual value is substituted for only i_{t-1} and the computed value of extrapolation equation for other exogenous variables.

$$y^F_t = \pi_I (\bar{i}_{t-1}, \hat{x}^o_t \mid \bar{z}_{1954:4}) \tag{14}$$

Simulation IV and V are prepared, in comparison with Simulation III, to extract separately the influences which cyclical deviations from the trends of O_{t-1} and i_{t-1} effectuate on the final solution. These comparisons are shown in Fig. 4.2.

ii) Interest Rate Policy and Business Cycles

The Japanese economy has experienced recessions several times in the post-war period, and various controversies have occurred in connection with the relation between these recessions and tight money policies.

They seem particularly to be controversies on interpretations of the phenomenon of recessions which occurred after adopting of tight money policies. Opinions expressed in these controversies seem to belong to either of the following speculations.

One is the theory of endogenously generated business cycle. This is the view which insists that, though the tight money policy taken when the business cycle was under the course of endogenous depression, surely gave a rise to the recession, the business cycle would intrinsicly generate a downswing without the tight money policy.

The other is a view of an exogenous generating business cycle, which insists that monetary policy causes directly the recession and that the recession would never occur unless the tight money policy had been.

In addition to the above two theories, the author would like to suggest, as a result of his simulations studies, that a resonance has occurred between the economic system and monetary policy. This idea will not contradict the two alternative theories mentioned above and will not reject them completely.

In the theory of oscillation, the following proposition concerning resonance is well known. If the period of the exogenous oscillation added to a certain oscillatory system coincides with the period of the inherent oscillation of the latter, or a fraction, i.e., $^1/_2$, $^1/_3$, ..., or more generally if it is an integral multiple of the period of the inherent oscillation, the resonance will necessarily occur without regard to its phase and amplitude. The amplitude of the oscillation will be rapidly amplified after a short transient process. If the system is linear, the amplitude will be infinite when both oscillations coincide completely[1]. In the case of

[1] The mechanism of resonance has been discussed in *R.G.D.Allen,* Mathematical Economics. Macmillan 1956, pp. 223–227 as follows: For example, in the *Hicks*-type second order difference equation model, *J.R.Hicks,* A Contribution to the Theory of the Trade Cycle. 1950, pp. 42 assume that autonomous investment A_t oscillates regularly according to a given sinusoidal function.

$$A_t = A_0 \, Cos\,(kt - k_0). \tag{1}$$

This is an exogenous oscillation of fixed period $2\pi/k$ and the fixed amplitude A_0 and the difference equation model can be written;

$$Y_t - aY_{t-1} + bY_{t-2} = A_t \tag{2}$$

where a and b are positive constants. The solution for Y_t given by (2) has inherent oscillations which are mildly damped, regular amplitude or mildly explosive and with a period greater than 4 intervals of time. Hence, the oscillatory term in the

the non-linear system, even if the period of oscillation to be added does not coincide with the inherent period, if the period of the exogenous oscillation is approximately equal to the inherent period, the period of the exogenous oscillation is "pulled in" to the synchronization with the period of the inherent oscillation and a resonance like phenomenon will occur. This law in physics requires us to concentrate our attention again on the periods of $\Pi_I(\hat{x}_t \mid \bar{z}_{1954:4})$, i.e., Simulation III and $\{p_2 D(\bar{i}_t - 1)\}$[2]. The author will focus our attention only on the *GNP* among solutions of each simulation in the following analyses, unless otherwise indicated.

In *A* of Fig. 4.3, the computed value of the equation (15.1) below is shown by a thick solid line and that of equation (15.2) by a thin dotted line.

$$(15.1) \qquad p_1 [D\{\bar{O}_{t-1}\} - a_{11}] + p_2 [D\{\bar{i}_{t-1}\} - a_{21}]$$

$$(15.2) \qquad D[\pi_I\{\bar{O}_{t-1}, \bar{i}_{t-1}, \hat{x}^o{}_t \mid \bar{z}_{1954:4}\}] - D[\pi_I(\hat{x}_t \mid \bar{z}_{1954:4})]$$

where a_{11} and a_{21} are the regression coefficients of the time variable of the extrapolation equation O_{t-1} and i_{t-1} respectively. In *B* of Fig. 4.3, the following equations are shown in the same way as the above,

$$(16.1) \qquad p_2 [D\{\bar{i}_{t-1}\} - a_{11}]$$

$$(16.2) \qquad D[\pi_I\{\bar{i}_{t-1}, \hat{x}^o{}_t \mid \bar{z}_{1954:4}\}] - D[\pi_I(\hat{x}_t \mid \bar{z}_{1954:4})]$$

and likewise in *C* of Fig. 4.3, the equations

$$(17.1) \qquad p_1 [D\{\bar{O}_{t-1}\} - a_{11}]$$

$$(17.2) \qquad D[\pi_I\{\bar{O}_{t-1}, \hat{x}^o{}_t \mid \bar{z}_{1954:4}\}] - D[\pi_I(\hat{x}_t \mid \bar{z}_{1954:4})]$$

are shown.

Each of the first equations in these three pairs of equations corresponds to the forced term of the exogenous oscillation, that is, a direct influence (hereinafter called "component"). Each of the second ones shows the direct and indirect influence of the exogenous oscillation

---

solution is $Av^t \, Cos\,(\theta t - \varepsilon)$ where v and θ are given in terms of a and b when $v = 1$ exactly, i.e., the inherent oscillation is regular, the general solution can be written;

$$(3) \qquad Y_t = A\,Cos\,(\theta t - \varepsilon) + \frac{A_o}{2\,(Cos\,k - Cos\,\theta)}\,Cos\,\{kt - (k_o - k)\}$$

(3) shows that the amplitude of Y_t oscillation is proportional to that of A_t oscillation. The multiplier is $\lambda = \dfrac{1}{2\,(Cos\,k - Cos\,\theta)}$

and λ increases as $k \to \theta$ and the forced and inherent oscillation tend to have the same period, the value of $\lambda \to \infty$. Hence, the amplitude of the Y_t oscillation increases indefinitely when the forced oscillation agrees in period with the inherent oscillation.

[2] Since the first coefficient of a reduced form corresponds to O_{t-1}, it may be written p_1. To the same manner, since the second coefficient does i_{t-1}, it can be written p_2.

Note that p_1 and p_2 are not column vectors but scalers forcussing on only the path over time of *GNP*.

Fig. 4.3 *Comparison of "Component" & "Factor"* by Simulation Analysis

Real value at constant price of 1955

(Unit: a billion yen)

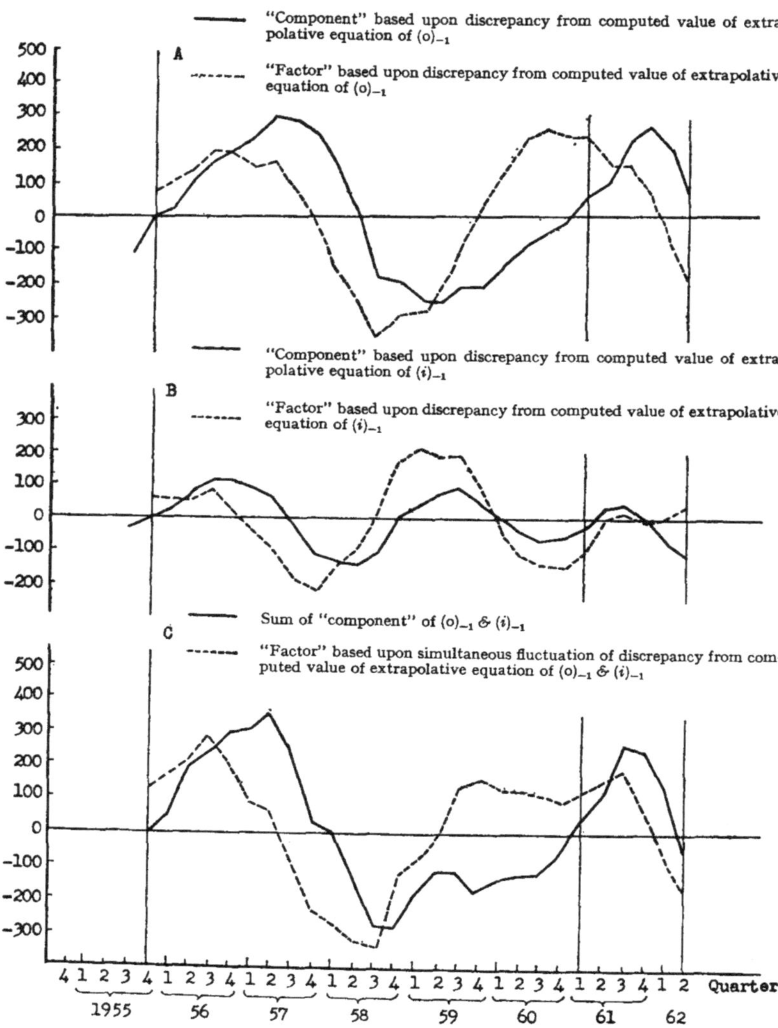

(hereinafter called "factor"). Subtracting "component" from "factor", the net indirect influence will be obtained. As is evident in Fig. 4.3, amplitudes of "component" and "factor" are slightly different in the case of O_{t-1}.

To the contrary, for i_{t-1}, the amplitude of "factor" is twice amplified in comparison with that of "component". Then, in comparison of the period of $\pi_I[\hat{x}_t \mid \bar{z}_{1954:4}]$ with that of $p_2[D\{\bar{i}_{t-1}\} - a_{21}]$, it is found that both of these periods are approximately three years. Judging from these results, the following conjectures may be made.

Since the period of $D\{i_{t-1}\}$ agrees with the intrinsic period of the economic system, the resonance phenomenon seems to occur and the change of i_{t-1} seems to give unexpectedly the great influence on the fluctuations of *GNP*.

From these conjectures, it may not be inappropriate to propose that the theory of a resonance effect of interest rate policy in the relation between the tight money policy and recession as is stated before.

The policy implications of this theory are as follows. The monetary policy in post-war Japan has had an amplified influence on the business cycle because the timing of the policy has accidentally or consciously agreed with the period of economic system. If the period of policy had been slightly different, there should have been no resonance effect and the effect of policies should at most have been to a degree as shown in (16.1). It should be noted, in this respect, that the effect of the policy depends critically on its timing (the period).

J.R.Hicks[1] and *R.G.D.Allen*[2] have mentioned that this resonance can occur in the simple model of business cycle, but so far no one has pointed out the resonance effect in the business cycles of the real world as a result of the analysis based on the econometric model.

It is the period of exogenous oscillation with the same period as the intrinsic period of economic system that has caused the resonance phenomenon. The resonance effect is not due to the phasing of the intrinsic and exogenous oscillations and the change of their amplitudes over time.

In order to make the conjecture more complete, it is necessary to confirm (a) whether the resonance effect will occur by giving the artificial wave, $D\{\tilde{i}_{t-1}\}$ which has the same period as that of the actual $D\{\bar{i}_{t-1}\}$ but different phasing and amplitude, and (b) whether the resonance effect will disappear in the case of an artificial $D\{\tilde{i}_{t-1}\}$ with the same initial phasing and the same amplitude as the actual $D\{\bar{i}_{t-1}\}$ but with a different length of period. If these points are confirmed, then it will be clear that the Japanese economy described by our model has the resonance phenomenon of the actual $D\{\bar{i}_{t-1}\}$. The artificial waves $D\{\tilde{i}_{t-1}\}$ used in experiments (a) and (b) are generated respectively by the equations (18.a) and (18.b), below.

(18.a) $$D\{\tilde{i}_{t-1}\} - \tilde{a}_{21} = A_t \, Cos\,(\overline{w}t + e)$$

[1] See *J.R.Hicks*, a.a.O.

[2] See *R.G.D.Allen*, a.a.O.

actual period: $2\,\pi/\bar{w} = 12$ quarters (3 years)

amplitude: $A_t = \bar{b}t + c_i \qquad i = 1, \ldots.., I$

phasing: $e_j \qquad j = 1, \ldots.., J$

where $\bar{a}_{21}$ is the regression coefficient of the extrapolation equation of i_{t-1}, therefore it is always constant.

The variable parameters in (18.a) are c and e. The bar on the parameter means that the parameter in question is constant.

(18.b) $$D\,\{\tilde{i}_{t-1}\} + \bar{a}_{21} = \bar{A}_t\, Cos\,(wt + \bar{e})$$

actual amplitude: $\bar{A}_t = \bar{b}t + \bar{c}$
actual initially phasing: $\bar{e}$

period: $2\,\pi/w_k \qquad k = 1, \ldots.., K$

where the various forms of w_k are considered. In addition, to experiments (a) and (b), experiment (c) was carried out, by giving the exponential function to w_t, in order to search the length of the period for which the resonance occurs.

(18.c) $$D\,\{\tilde{i}_{t-1}\} = \bar{a}_{21} = A_t\, Cos\,(w_t t + e)$$ $$w_t = \bar{h}\, exp\,[\bar{g}t]$$

The value of the parameters b, c_i, e_j, w_k, h and g are determined so that the pseudo-realistic wave to be defined below approximates the actual $D\,\{\tilde{i}_{t-1}\}$ as much as possible. In this case, the least squares estimates are used for the respective parameters,

(19)

$\bar{b} =$	$-\,0.421 \times 10^{-2}$	(percentage / 4 quarters)
$\bar{c} =$	0.482	(percentage / 4 quarters)
$\bar{e} =$	0.270×10^{1}	(radian)
$\bar{w} =$	3×8	(radian / 4 quarters)
$\bar{h} =$	0.193×10^{2}	(scaling factor)
$\bar{g} =$	$-\,0.224 \times 10^{-1}$	(log (radian) / 4 quarters)

The unit of the changes of parameters in experiments (a), (b) and (c) above are respectively,

(20) $$\Delta\bar{c} = 0.5 \times 10^{-1}$$ $$\Delta\bar{e} = \pi$$ $$\Delta\bar{w} = 1 \times 8\pi$$

The experiments (a), (b) and (c) are carried out by Simulation VI–a, b and c, respectively. These simulations are the same as i_{t-1} of Simulation V, i.e., $\Pi_I\,\{\tilde{i}_{t-1},\ \hat{x}^{o}{}_t \mid z_{1954:4}\}$, except that $\tilde{i}_{t-1}$ is substituted for. Therefore, these simulations are defined according to the specifications of this i_{t-1}.

Experiment 0: (pseudo-realistic wave (1): LS estimate $\bar{b}$, $\bar{c}$, $\bar{e}$ and $\bar{w}$ in the expression (19) are substituted for the expression (18.a) or (18.b). This experiment is used for the basis of comparison with the other experiments.)

Simulation VI–a (changes of amplitude and phasing)

(21) $$\tilde{i}_{t-1} = D^{-1}. \{a_{21} + A_t \, Cos \, (\bar{w}t + e)\}$$

where $A_t = \bar{f}_t + c$

Experiment 1: (decreasing amplitude: $c = \bar{c} - \Delta\bar{c}$)
Experiment 2: (increasing amplitude: $c = \bar{c} + \Delta\bar{c}$)
Experiment 3: (leading phase: $e = \bar{e} + \Delta\bar{e}$)
Experiment 4: (more leading phase: $e = \bar{e} + 2\Delta\bar{e}$
Simulation VI–b (changes of period length)

(22) $$\tilde{i}_{t-1} = D^{-1} \{\bar{a}_{21} + \bar{A}_t \, Cos \, (wt + \bar{e})\}$$

Experiment 5: (1 year period: $w = \bar{w} - 2\Delta\bar{w}$)
Experiment 6: (2 years period: $w = \bar{w} - \Delta\bar{w}$)[1]
Experiment 7: (4 years period: $w = \bar{w} + \Delta\bar{w}$)
Experiment 8: (5 years period: $w = \bar{w} + 2\Delta\bar{w}$)
Simulation VI–c (monotonically decreasing period)

(23) $$\tilde{i}_{t-1} = D^{-1}. \{\bar{a}_{21} + \bar{A}_t \, Cos \, (w^*(t) \, . \, t + \bar{e})\}$$
$$w^*(t) = \bar{h}e^{\bar{g}t}$$

Experiment 0': (pseudo-realistic wave (2)):
(This is the one which substitutes the least squares estimates of (15), $\bar{b}$, $\bar{c}$, $\bar{e}$, $\bar{h}$ and $\bar{g}$ for Equation (19).)

Experiment 1': (decreasing amplitude: $c = \bar{c} - \Delta\bar{c}$)
Experiment 2': (increasing amplitude: $c = \bar{c} + \Delta\bar{c}$)
Experiment 3': (leading phasing: $e = \bar{e} + \Delta\bar{e}$)
Experiment 4': (more leading phasing: $e = \bar{e} + 2\Delta\bar{e}$)

The author judged whether the resonance phenomenon has occurred or not by comparing each of differences of experimental Simulation VI, (a), (b) and (c) from Simulation III, i.e., $\pi_I \{\hat{x}_t \mid \bar{z}_{1954:4}\}$ with $P_2[D \{\tilde{i}_{t-1}\} - \bar{a}_{21}]$.

The results are shown in Table 4.1.

It is made clear, by the above experiments, that when $D \{\tilde{i}_{t-1}\}$ is made the wave with the actual period, there has been caused the resonance phenomenon even if the amplitude and the phasing had been different from actual ones[2]. In addition, it has proved, from the monotonically decreasing case of the period, that the oscillation with the period of three quarters has an amplifying effect of more than 3.5 times. Moreover, in the case of the periods which are integral multiples

[1] In case of a two-years' period: Simulation VI (b), it was found to be a non-resonance case. In such a case, the author tried to test four cases in which amplitudes and phasing differ as examined in (a), but all four cases had no resonance as was expected.

[2] It should be particularly noted that resonance phenomena may be caused by oscillations of all other exogenous variables as well as those of i_{t-1}, if they have the period equivalent to the period of the inherent oscillation of this model. Therefore, resonance phenomena in the Japanese economy expressed by our models were caused by other exogenous variables as well as i_{t-1}.

of 7×3 quarters, i.e., three years (4×3 quarters), near four years (6×3 quarters) and near five years (7×3 quarters), the resonance seems to be caused according to the result of (b) of Simulation VI. However, it was difficult to judge whether or not the resonance was caused definitely in each case of 2×3 quarters, 3×3 quarters and 5×3 quarters, so far as these experiments are concerned. Since only a half of a cycle with the period of integral multiple was observed, it could not be said definitely that the resonance has been caused, even if the amplitude was amplified, say, more than 1.5 times in the case of 3×3 quarters[1].

Table 4.1

Results of Experimental Simulations for generating resonance phenomena in the different situations

Simulation VI Experi-ment 0	Pseudo-realistic Wave (with 3 yr. period)		Parameter $w = \bar{w}$ $c = \bar{c}$ $e = \bar{e}$	Existence of resonance phenomenon	
				resonance	Amplifing multiplier
Simulation VI–(a)	amplitude	decreasing increasing	$c = \bar{c} - \Delta c$ $c = \bar{c} + \Delta c$	resonance resonance	$\lambda = 2.0$ $\lambda = 2.0$
	phasing	leading further leading	$e = \bar{e} + \Delta e$ $e = \bar{e} + 2\Delta e$	resonance resonance	$\lambda = 2.0$ $\lambda = 2.0$
Simulation VI–(b)	Period	1 year 2 years 4 years 5 years	$w = \bar{w} - 2\Delta w$ $w = \bar{w} - 1\Delta w$ $w = \bar{w} + 1\Delta w$ $w = \bar{w} + 2\Delta w$	no no* resonance resonance	$\lambda = 1.0$ $\lambda = 1.0$ $\lambda = 2.0$ $\lambda = 2.0$
Simulation VI–(c)	Pseudo-realistic Wave with monotonic decreasing period		$w^*(g, h)$ $c = \bar{c}$ $e = \bar{e}$	The length of period and maximum multi-plier (unit period = 3 quarters = u.p.)	
				4 u.p.	1 u.p.
	Experiment 0			$\lambda_1 = 2.0$	$\lambda_2 = 3.7$
	amplitude	decreasing increasing	$c = \bar{c} - \Delta c$ $c = \bar{c} + \Delta c$	$\lambda_1 = 2.0$ $\lambda_1 = 2.0$	$\lambda_2 = 3.5$ $\lambda_2 = 3.8$
	phasing	leading further laeding	$e = \bar{e} + \Delta e$ $e = \bar{e} + 2\Delta e$	$\lambda_1 = 2.0$ $\lambda_1 = 2.0$	$\lambda_2 = 3.6$ $\lambda_2 = 3.8$

[1] To be certain of this, such experiments as in Simulation IV (a) would be required to be made by fixing the period twice, three times and five times as long as three quarters.

On the contrary, it seems to support this conjecture that there is no resonance in the cases of a two-years' period which is not an integral-multiple of three quarters[1].

iii) Relation of Monetary Policy and the Component of i_{t-1}

In this section, the change of the average of agreed interest on loans and discounts i_{t-1} has so far been regarded as the monetary policy. It may be necessary to add some explanation for this. First, the official rate of interest is considered as a representative index of monetary policy. If we examine the relation between the official rate of interest and the agreed interest, it is found that two interest rates show extremely similar movements as is shown in Fig. 4.4. Although they differ in amplitude, the definite similarity in period and phasing can be seen.

From the sensible reaction of the agreed interest rate i_{t-1} on the official interest rate, the former is also regarded as a representative variable which reflects the monetary policy. Therefore, i_{t-1} may be treated here as a quasi-mean-variable.

5. Simulations of Fiscal Policies

i) Effects of Public Expenditures

A sketch of the mixed model and the private sector model is shown in Fig. 5.1 by selecting only the variables directly related to the fiscal policies. As seen from the figure, the private sector model is included in the mixed model.

Usually, the "multiplier effect" is defined to be the ratio of the marginal increase in *GNP* to the marginal increase of the Governmental expenditures in the limit of propagation. However, the simulation we can perform cannot but be limited to the short-run iterative process. For the convenience of practical use, it will be sufficient if the time path of the effect of the various policies could be known in the finite interval in which the structure indicated by the model does not vary. Therefore, the numerical value within such an interval in which the time path of policy effect is comparatively stable is to be defined as a dynamic multiplier.

The notation "=" on each increment of the variable shows that the variable is exogenous in the model, and the "—" denotes endogenous one. In case of operating the variable with "—", the constant term in

[1] If there is no nonlinear term Max $[Av(c)]$ in our models and imaginary roots can be obtained by the suitable numercial method, it would be possible to precisely discuss the preceeding matters by solving the characteristic root of the characteristic equation in the high order simultaneous difference equation system. If the problem of the existence of inherent oscillations in the system was clarified, a periodical analysis of it could be carried out more exactly.

Fig. 4.4 *Fluctuations of Official Rate & Average Agreed Rate of Interest on Loans and Discounts (i)*

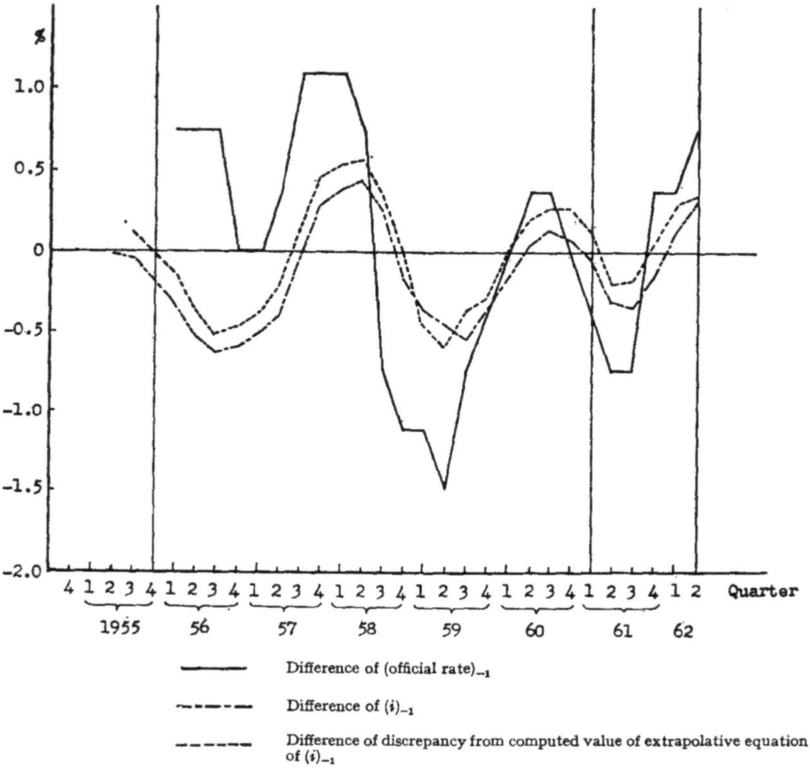

the reduced form to explain the variable is to be shifted as much as required.

The simulations performed on the following analysis are to be explained.

Simulation VII (mixed model)

(24) $$\pi_I\,(\bar{G}_{Ft} \pm \Delta\bar{\bar{G}}_{IF},\ \bar{x}^o{}_t \mid \bar{z}_{1954:4}) - \pi_I\,(\bar{x}_t \mid \bar{z}_{1954:4})$$

The initial period is the same fourth quarter of 1954 as follow before. The second term of (24) is Simulation I. In addition, $\pi_I(G_t \pm \Delta\bar{G}, \bar{x}_t \mid \bar{z}_{1954:4})$ is performed, and a similar treatment is made.

Simulation VIII (private sector model)[1]

(25) $$\pi_{II}\,(\bar{G}_t \pm \Delta\bar{\bar{G}},\ \bar{x}^o{}_t \mid \bar{z}_{1954:4}) - \pi_{II}\,(\bar{x}_t \mid \bar{z}_{1954:4})$$

The initial period is the same as the above.

[1] Refer to the private sector model in Appendix A. 2 (ii).

Fig. 5.1
(Private & Public Mixed Model)

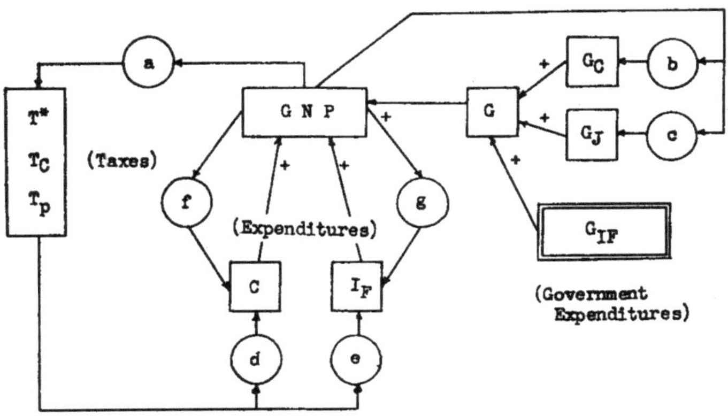

$G = G_C + G_J + \bar{G}_{IF}$

G: Government Expenditures

G_C: Government Consumption

G_J: Increase in Inventory Stock of Government Sector

G_{IF}: Government Investment

(Rough Sketch of Private Model)

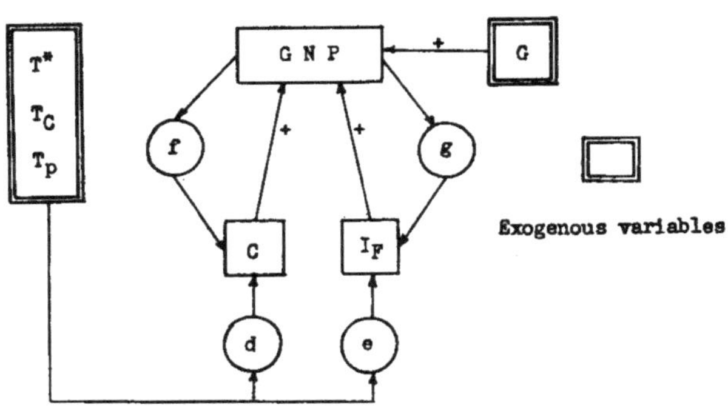

The second term of (25) corresponds to Simulation I in the private sector model.

$\Delta\bar{G}_{IF}$ and $\Delta\bar{G}$ are set as $\Delta\bar{G}_{IF} = \Delta\bar{G}$, which is 20% of the average value of G_{IF} in the four quarters in 1950. This value is continuously added to the actual value of G_{IFt} and G_t

Consequently, it should be noted that, in shifting the constant term as much as $\Delta\bar{G}$ to shift the Government purchases of goods and services G which is an endogenous variable in the mixed model, the change $\Delta G(\Delta\bar{G})$ caused in the endogenous variable G in the solution of the model does not always correspond to the shift $\Delta\bar{G}$.

Thus, observing the mixed model, the dynamic policy effect of the Government purchases on GNP is given by taking up the ratio of $\Delta\ GNP(\Delta\bar{G})$ and $\Delta G(\Delta\bar{G})$. This is called the first dynamic policy effect $\mu_I(\Delta\bar{G})$ in the mixed model. In case of shifting the Government investment G_{IFt}, which is an endogenous variable in the mixed model, as much as $\Delta\bar{\bar{G}}_{IF}$, the Government consumption G_c, the Government inventory investment G_{Jt} and therefore their sum G_t shift as much as $\Delta G(\Delta\bar{\bar{G}}_{IF})$. The dynamic policy-effect of the Government purchases increment on GNP is measured by taking up the ratio of this and $\Delta GNP(\Delta\bar{\bar{G}}_{IF})$. This is called the second dynamic policy effect $\mu_I(\Delta\bar{\bar{G}}_{IF})$ in the mixed model.

On the other hand, in the private sector model, since G is not disaggregated into G_{IF}, G_J, and G_c, G is the only exogenous variable which is operated.

Therefore, in the private sector model, the ratio of $\Delta\bar{\bar{G}}$ and $\Delta GNP(\Delta\bar{\bar{G}})$ is observed. This is called the dynamic policy effect $(\mu_I(\Delta\bar{\bar{G}}))$ of the private sector model.

Table 5.1

	Mixed Model	Private Model
(1)	$\mu_I(\Delta\bar{G}) = \{\Delta GNP(\Delta\bar{G}) / \Delta G(\Delta\bar{G})\}$	
(2)	$\mu_I(\Delta\bar{\bar{G}}_{IF}) = \{\Delta GNP(\Delta\bar{\bar{G}}_{IF}) / \Delta G(\Delta\bar{\bar{G}}_{IF})\}$	$\mu_{II}(\Delta\bar{\bar{G}}) = \{\Delta GNP(\Delta\bar{\bar{G}}) / \Delta\bar{\bar{G}}\}$
(3)	$\mu'_I(\Delta\bar{\bar{G}}_{IF}) = \{\Delta GNP(\Delta\bar{\bar{G}}_{IF}) / \Delta\bar{\bar{G}}_{IF}\}$	

For the comparison with the private sector model, the second ratio in the mixed model will be more realistic, because, firstly, the first ratio implies that the Government investment G_{IF} is not varied at all in case of shifting G as much as $\Delta\bar{G}$ though G_c and G_J changes with G. Secondly, in the second ratio, it is implied that G is varied provided that there are the changes of G_c and G_J corresponding to the change of G_{IF}. This ratio is measured from the first quarter to the fourth quarter of 1958 except the transient period immediately after simulation has started. See shown Table 5.2.

In the table, $\mu_I\ (\Delta\bar{\bar{G}}_{IF})$ shows the most plausible value, while $\mu_I\ (\Delta\bar{G})$ is so small as to be meaningless. $\mu_{II}\ (\Delta\bar{G})$ showed a considerably high value.

ii) Measurement of the Stabilizing Effect of Fiscal Policies

The tax rates in Japan, i.e., rates in the income tax, the corporate tax and the indirect tax has been cut almost every year since 1950. It

Table 5.2

	$\mu_I(\Delta\bar{G})$	$\mu_I(\Delta\bar{\bar{G}}_{IF})$	$\mu'_I(\Delta\bar{\bar{G}}_{IF})$		$\mu_{II}(\Delta\bar{\bar{G}})$	
1958:1	—0.1	3.4	4.0	4.2	5.5	5.3
1958:2	0.6	3.1	6.5	3.9	5.6	5.2
1958:3	0.1	3.5	4.7	4.0	5.7	5.2
1958:4	0.6	3.1	3.8	6.5	5.7	5.0
	$\pm\Delta\bar{G}$ symmetric effect	$\pm\Delta\bar{\bar{G}}_{IF}$ symmetric effect	$+\Delta\bar{\bar{G}}_{IF}$	$-\Delta\bar{\bar{G}}_{IF}$	$+\Delta\bar{G}$	$-\Delta\bar{G}$

can hardly be said that the tax rates in Japan are fixed with the exception of the comparatively stable corporate tax rate. This kind of tax reduction policy is recently regarded as the favorable target of the tax reduction policy in United States economy by *Burnes* and *Samuelson*. As a result of the reduction in tax rates carried out in this way, the natural increase in government revenue, which is expected without a tax cut, is automatically returned to the private sector.

There are some opinions of specialists in fiscal policies that such a radical change of tax rates spoils the stabilizing effect[1] of the fiscal structure.

It is made clear, however, that the striking stabilizing force in the taxation system with changes in tax rates still exists from the measured value of the stabilizing effect (β) to be defined below.

See Table 5.3

(26) $$\beta = [1 - \{\mu_I(\Delta\bar{\bar{G}}_{IF}) \mid \mu_{II}(\Delta\bar{\bar{G}})\}]$$

Table 5.3

		1958:1	1958:2	1958:3	1958:4
β	$\Delta > 0$	0.384	0.452	0.379	0.454
	$\Delta < 0$	0.355	0.410	0.318	0.379

[1] The term "automatic" has usually been used as the one with respect to the stabilizing force of the fixed tax rate. However, the dynamic features on the stabilizing force of the tax function shown in our model shall be measured.

Appendix A

Variables & Equations of "Mixed Model" and "Private Model"

A–1 Notation of Variables

Subscript (— 1) means "preceding period". Quarterly data without seasonal adjustment are used

Notation & Unit (** stock quantity)		Deflator[b] (1955 = 100)	Data Source & Calculation Basis
A = Proprietor's income	(a billion yen)	Imputed price index numbers[a]	Economic Planning Agency, *White Paper on National Accounts*
$Av(GNP^*)$ = Four quarters moving average of the past gross private income	(a billion yen)		GNP^*
C = Private consumption expenditure	(a billion yen)	General price index numbers of consumers' goods	*White Paper on National Accounts*
D_G = Government capital consumption allowances	(a billion yen)	Price index numbers of producers' goods	*White Paper on National Accounts*
D_H = Personal residential consumption allowances	(a billion yen)	Price index numbers of producers' goods	*White Paper on National Accounts*
D_F = Private equipment consumption allowances	(a billion yen)	Price index numbers of producers' goods	*White Paper on National Accounts*
E = Export	(a billion yen)	Unit value index numbers of export	*White Paper on National Accounts*
e = Statistical discrepancy[c]	(a billion yen)		Recalculated on real base
G = Government purchase of goods and services	(a billion yen)		Appendix A–2, identity (29) of (ii)
G_C = Government consumption	(a billion yen)	General price index numbers of consumers' goods	*White Paper on National Accounts*
G_{IF} = Government investment in fixed assets	(a billion yen)	Price index numbers of producers' goods	

Notation & Unit (** stock quantity)	Deflator[b] (1955 = 100)	Data Source & Calculation Basis
G_J = Increase in inventory stock of Government sector (a billion yen)	Price index numbers of inventory stocks	*White Paper on National Accounts*
GNP = Gross national product (a billion yen)		Appendix A–2, identity (19) of (ii)
GNP^* = Gross private income (a billion yen)		Appendix A–2, identity (20) of (ii)
H = Contribution by Government to social insurance (a billion yen)	Imputed price index numbers	*White Paper on National Accounts*
i = Averages of agreed interest rates on loans and discounts[d] (%)		The Bank of Japan, *Economic Statistics of Japan*
I_F = Private investment in producers' durable equipment (Private fixed investment) (a billion yen)	Price index numbers of producers' goods	*White Paper on National Accounts*
I_H = Personal residential housing construction (a billion yen)	Price index numbers of producers' goods	*White Paper on National Accounts*
J = Increase in inventory stock of private sector (Inventory investment) (a billion yen)	Price index numbers of inventory stocks	*White Paper on National Accounts*
K_F = Stock of capital in the form of producers' durable equipment** (a billion yen)[e]	Price index numbers of producers' goods	Calculated from identity (25) of (ii), Appendix A–2
K_H = Stock of capital in the form of residential houses** (a billion yen)[e]	Price index numbers of producers' goods	Calculated from identity (24) of (ii), Appendix A–2
K_J = Private inventory stock** (a billion yen)[e]	Price index numbers of producers' goods	Calculated from identity (23) of (ii), Appendix A–2
L_H = Loanable funds provided for residential housing construction by government (a billion yen)	Price index numbers of producers' goods	Data of Economic Planning Agency

Notation & Unit (** stock quantity)	Deflator[b] (1955 = 100)	Data Source & Calculation Basis
M = *Import* (a billion yen)	Unit value index number of import	*White Paper on National Accounts*
$Max\ [Av(C)]$ = maximum among the four quarters moving average of past personal consumption expenditure (a billion yen)		Calculated from C $Max\ [Av(C)] = \underset{T \leqq t}{Max}\left[\frac{C_{t-1}+C_{t-2}+C_{t-3}+C_{t-4}}{4}\right]$
M_W = World trade transacted quantity index number (%)	Unit value index number of world trade	*United Nations: Monthly Bulletin of Statistics*
O = Outstanding orders received for machinery (a billion yen)		*Economic Statistics of Japan*
P = Non-labor, non-proprietor's private income (a billion yen)		Calculated from identity (21) of (ii), Appendix A–2
P_C = Corporate income (a billion yen)	Imputed price index numbers	*White Paper on National Accounts*
Q_i = Dummy variables to show seasonal shifts		Q_i is 1 when i — *th* quarter of the year, and 0 when except i — *th* quarter of the year
S_C = Retained corporate profit increment (a billion yen)	Imputed price index numbers	*White Paper on National Accounts*
$S_D = T_G + D_G + e$ (a billion yen)		Calculated from right side of left equation
t = Time variable (where the first quarter of 1952 is to be 1.)		
T^* = Indirect tax minus subsidies (a billion yen)	Imputed price index numbers	*White Paper on National Accounts*

Notation & Unit (** stock quantity)		Deflator[b] (1955 = 100)	Data Source & Calculation Basis
T_C = Corporate tax	(a billion yen)	Imputed price index numbers	*White Paper on National Accounts*
T_G = Surplus of Government enterprises, etc.	(a billion yen)	Imputed price index numbers	*White Paper on National Accounts*
T_P = Personal tax	(a billion yen)	Imputed price index numbers	*White Paper on National Accounts*
T_R = Government transfer expenditure	(a billion yen)	Imputed price index numbers	*White Paper on National Accounts*
W = Compensation of employees	(a billion yen)	Imputed price index numbers	*White Paper on National Accounts*
Y_d = Disposable income	(a billion yen)		Calculated from identity (22) of (ii), Appendix A–2

[a] Imputed price index numbers = Nominal gross national product ÷ real gross national product (Calculated from identity (19)).

[b] Deflator of each variable is based on the data of National Income Department of Economic Planning Agency. But unit value of index number of world trade is calculated from *United Nations Monthly Bulletin of Statistics*, and the standard year is 1953 = 100.

[c] These are not the real values of nominal statistical discrepancy in *White Paper on National Accounts*.

[d] Average value of 3 months = quarter value.

[e] Calculated by each identity with the initial value of stock quantity in the statement of assets at the end of 1955 in *Structure of National Wealth of Japan* compiled under the supervision of *Dr. Ichiro Nakayama* (Toyo Keizai Shinpo Sha Co., Ltd., 1959).

A–2 Structural Equations and Identities

Unit of each variable is a billion yen (contact price of 1955 fiscal year). But as to i and M_W is %. The Observation period is from the fourth quarter of 1953 to the first quarter of 1955. The number in ( ) is the standard deviation of estimates. $\hat{R}$, $\hat{S}$, d, are respectively as follows. $\hat{R}$ = Multiple correlation coefficient adjusted with degrees of freedom, $\hat{S}$ = Standard deviation of residual adjusted with degree of freedom, d = *von Neumann* ratio.

(i) Structural Equations (Two-stage Least Squares Estimate)

Model I Private & Public Mixed Model (the number of equation: 18)
II Private Model (the number of equation: 12)

a) Private Sector (12)

Private consumption function	(1) I $C = 68.6 + \underset{(0.0563)}{0.265}\, Y_d + \underset{(0.0873)}{0.678}\, Max\,[A_v(C)] - \underset{(12.6)}{24.7}\, Q_2 - \underset{(15.6)}{50.0}\, Q_3 + \underset{(39.2)}{49.2}\, Q_4$ $\hat{R} = 0.995 \quad \hat{S} = 20.8 \quad d = 1.77$ (1) II $C = 88.4 + \underset{(0.0661)}{0.295}\, Y_d + \underset{(0.102)}{0.634}\, Max\,[A_v(C)] - \underset{(13.2)}{28.1}\, Q_2 - \underset{(17.1)}{55.9}\, Q_3 + \underset{(45.5)}{29.5}\, Q_4$ $\hat{R} = 0.995 \quad \hat{S} = 20.8 \quad d = 1.80$
Private residential construction function	(2) I $I_H = -31.2 + \underset{(0.00401)}{0.0470}\, Y_d + \underset{(0.715)}{2.07}\, L_{H-2} - \underset{(3.47)}{0.504}\, Q_2 - \underset{(2.82)}{0.562}\, Q_3 - \underset{(3.84)}{20.9}\, Q_4$ $\hat{R} = 0.954 \quad \hat{S} = 5.29 \quad d = 2.13$ (2) II $I_H = -31.7 + \underset{(0.00406)}{0.0475}\, Y_d + \underset{(0.718)}{2.02}\, L_{H-2} - \underset{(3.48)}{0.397}\, Q_2 - \underset{(2.83)}{0.601}\, Q_3 - \underset{(3.86)}{21.2}\, Q_4$ $\hat{R} = 0.953 \quad \hat{S} = 5.29 \quad d = 2.14$
Private investment in producer's durable equipment function	(3) I $I_F = -7.73 + \underset{(0.138)}{0.543}\, (P_C - T_C) + \underset{(0.00653)}{0.0667}\, K_{F-1} + \underset{(0.150)}{0.820}\, (P_C - T_C)_{-3} - \underset{(12.8)}{9.64}\, Q_2 + \underset{(12.7)}{54.8}\, Q_3 + \underset{(12.4)}{62.0}\, Q_4$ $\hat{R} = 0.992 \quad \hat{S} = 24.4 \quad d = 2.02$ (3) II $I_F = -171 + \underset{(0.137)}{0.551}\, (P_C - T_C) + \underset{(0.00652)}{0.0664}\, K_{F-1} + \underset{(0.150)}{0.817}\, (P_C - T_C)_{-3} - \underset{(12.8)}{9.53}\, Q_2 + \underset{(12.7)}{54.8}\, Q_3 + \underset{(12.4)}{62.1}\, Q_4$ $\hat{R} = 0.992 \quad \hat{S} = 24.5 \quad d = 2.02$

Import function	(4) I $M = 627 + \underset{(0.0389)}{0.430 I_F} + \underset{(0.0366)}{0.134 J} - \underset{(18.3)}{52.0\, i_{-1}} + \underset{(12.0)}{1.90\, Q_2} - \underset{(11.5)}{46.1\, Q_3} - \underset{(13.2)}{70.1\, Q_4}$	$\hat{R} = 0.978$ $\hat{S} = 22.0$ $d = 1.40$
	(4) II $M = 619 + \underset{(0.0386)}{0.440 I_F} + \underset{(0.0349)}{0.111 J} - \underset{(18.2)}{51.3\, i_{-1}} + \underset{(11.9)}{4.49\, Q_2} - \underset{(11.4)}{46.7\, Q_3} - \underset{(12.9)}{66.3\, Q_4}$	$\hat{R} = 0.979$ $\hat{S} = 21.8$ $d = 11.8$
Export function	(5) I, (5) II $E = -221 + \underset{(53.7)}{367\, M_W} + \underset{(0.00494)}{0.00790\, K_{F-1}} + \underset{(7.38)}{2.44\, Q_2} + \underset{(7.12)}{27.2\, Q_3} + \underset{(7.78)}{23.3\, Q_4}$	$\hat{R} = 0.980$ $\hat{S} = 13.7$ $d = 1.97$
Compensation of employees function	(6) I $W = -29.0 + \underset{(0.0107)}{0.411\, GNP^*} + \underset{(15.1)}{89.4\, Q_2} + \underset{(15.1)}{33.3\, Q_3} + \underset{(15.8)}{17.2\, Q_4}$	$\hat{R} = 0.991$ $\hat{S} = 29.1$ $d = 1.15$
	(6) II $W = -27.2 + \underset{(0.0108)}{0.410\, GNP^*} + \underset{(15.1)}{89.4\, Q_2} + \underset{(15.1)}{33.5\, Q_3} + \underset{(15.8)}{17.7\, Q_4}$	$\hat{R} = 0.987$ $\hat{S} = 29.1$ $d = 1.15$
Corporate profit function	(7) I $P_C = -1.49 + \underset{(0.0604)}{0.635\, P} + \underset{(0.0865)}{0.176\, P_{C-1}}$	$\hat{R} = 0.992$ $\hat{S} = 10.7$ $d = 1.46$
	(7) II $P_C = -1.48 + \underset{(0.0600)}{0.642\, P} + \underset{(0.0859)}{0.166\, P_{C-1}}$	$\hat{R} = 0.993$ $\hat{S} = 10.7$ $d = 1.41$
Retained corporate profit	(8) I $S_C = -156 + \underset{(0.0481)}{0.822\, (P_C - T_C)} + \underset{(0.101)}{0.957\, (P_C - T_C - S_C)_{-1}} + \underset{(8.26)}{14.5\, i_{-1}}$	$\hat{R} = 0.986$ $\hat{S} = 10.0$ $d = 1.10$
	(8) II $S_C = -161 + \underset{(0.0478)}{0.826\, (P_C - T_C)} + \underset{(0.101)}{0.954\, (P_C - T_C - S_C)_{-1}} + \underset{(8.23)}{15.1\, i_{-1}}$	$\hat{R} = 0.988$ $\hat{S} = 10.0$ $d = 1.11$
Proprietor's income function	(9) I $A = 367 + \underset{(0.00986)}{0.0879\, GNP^*} - \underset{(13.9)}{51.5\, Q_2} + \underset{(13.9)}{70.7\, Q_3} + \underset{(14.5)}{262\, Q_4}$	$\hat{R} = 0.985$ $\hat{S} = 26.7$ $d = 1.12$
	(9) II $A = 369 + \underset{(0.00988)}{0.0866\, GNP^*} - \underset{(13.9)}{51.6\, Q_2} + \underset{(13.9)}{70.8\, Q_3} + \underset{(14.5)}{263\, Q_4}$	$\hat{R} = 0.983$ $\hat{S} = 26.7$ $d = 1.23$

Private residential capital consumption allowances function	(10) I $D_H = -50.6 + 0.0120\, Y_d + 0.0269 \left(\frac{K_H + K_{H-1}}{2}\right) - 0.341\, Q_2 - 1.73\, Q_3 - 8.46\, Q_4$ (0.00760) (0.00993) (1.57) (1.98) (5.18) $\hat{R} = 0.966$ $\hat{S} = 2.53$ $d = 0.596$ (10) II $D_H = -42.7 + 0.0179\, Y_d + 0.0193 \left(\frac{K_H + K_{H-1}}{2}\right) - 1.02\, Q_2 - 2.89\, Q_3 - 12.4\, Q_4$ (0.00946) (0.0123) (1.72) (2.28) (6.39) $\hat{R} = 0.968$ $\hat{S} = 2.59$ $d = 0.758$
Private equipment capital consumption allowances function	(11) I $D_F = -388 + 0.0392 \left(\frac{K_F + K_{F-1}}{2}\right) - 8.63\, Q_2 + 15.6\, Q_3 + 42.0\, Q_4$ $\hat{R} = 0.991$ $\hat{S} = 8.86$ $d = 1.72$ (0.000995) (4.60) (4.59) (4.43) (11) II same as (11) I
Inventory stock function	(12) I, (12) II $K_J = 977 + 1.65\, A_v (GNP^*) + 0.950\, O_{-1} - 211\, i_{-1} + 54.3\, Q_2 - 14.7\, Q_3 + 84.1\, Q_4$ (0.0972) (0.174) (101) (52.3) (52.2) (50.4) $\hat{R} = 0.995$ $\hat{S} = 10.1$ $d = 1.36$

b) Government Sector (6)

Government consumption function	(13) I $G_C = 225 + 0.0695\, GNP - 259\, Q_2 - 207\, Q_3 - 117\, Q_4$ $\hat{R} = 0.975$ $\hat{S} = 27.6$ $d = 1.83$ (0.00983) (14.7) (14.4) (15.0)
Government inventory investment function	(14) I $G_J = -73.2 + 0.0877\, G + 0.375\, \Delta G + 124\, Q_2 - 29.7\, Q_3 + 42.7\, Q_4$ $\hat{R} = 0.885$ $\hat{S} = 45.9$ $d = 1.70$ (0.0808) (0.0780) (35.1) (40.7) (38.4)
Indirect enterprise tax function	(15) I $T^* = 89.8 + 0.0294\, GNP + 3.71\, t - 14.7\, Q_2 - 12.4\, Q_3 - 21.1\, Q_4$ $\hat{R} = 0.965$ $\hat{S} = 12.8$ $d = 1.74$ (0.0133) (0.792) (7.68) (7.00) (10.8)
Personal income tax function	(16) I $T_P = 82.2 + 0.0272\, W + 0.0552\, A - 55.0\, Q_2 - 29.3\, Q_3 - 59.4\, Q_4$ $\hat{R} = 0.907$ $\hat{S} = 10.2$ $d = 0.962$ (0.0176) (0.0728) (7.37) (7.10) (19.7)
Corporate tax function	(17) I $T_C = 3.67 + 1.09\, t + 0.237\, P_{C-1} + 20.1\, Q_2 - 5.31\, Q_3 + 20.5\, Q_4$ $\hat{R} = 0.961$ $\hat{S} = 9.18$ $d = 1.93$ (0.389) (0.0364) (4.79) (4.76) (4.63)
Contribution by Government social insurance function	(18) I $H = 6.10 + 0.0166\, GNP^* + 0.905\, t - 9.13\, Q_2 - 5.16\, Q_3 - 10.0\, Q$ $\hat{R} = 0.982$ $\hat{S} = 3.20$ $d = 2.01$ (0.00508) (0.291) (1.67) (1.79) (3.60)

(ii) Identities (12)

Gross national production	(19) I, (13) II: $GNP = C + I_H + I_F + J + G + E - M$
Private national income	(20) I, (14) II: $GNP^* = GNP - (T_G + D_G + e)$
non-wage, non-proprietor's Private income	(21) I, (15) II: $P = GNP - T^* - D_F - D_H - W - A - (T_G + D_G + e)$
Disposable income	(22) I $Y_d = GNP - T^* - D_F - D_H - S_C - T_P - T_C - H - (T_G + D_G + e) + T_R$ (16) II $Y_d = GNP - D_F - D_H - S_C - (T^* + T_P + T_C + H + T_G + D_G + e - T_R)$
Increase in private inventory stock	(23) I, (17) II: $J = K_J - K_{J-1}$
Private residential stock	(24) I, (18) II: $K_H = I_H - D_H + K_{H-1}$
Private equipment stock	(25) I, (19) II: $K_F = I_F - D_F + K_{F-1}$
Other Identities	(26) I, (20) II: $\left(\frac{K_H + K_{H-1}}{2}\right) = \left(\frac{K_H}{2}\right) + \left(\frac{K_{H-1}}{2}\right)$ (27) I, (21) II: $\left(\frac{K_F + K_{F-1}}{2}\right) = \left(\frac{K_F}{2}\right) + \left(\frac{K_{F-1}}{2}\right)$ (28) I, (22) II: $(P_C - T_C) = P_C - T_C$
Government expenditures	(29) I $G = G_C + G_{IF} + G_J$
Increment of Government expenditures	(30) I $\Delta G = G - G_{-1}$

A–3 Extrapolation Equations of Exogenous Variables

I	II
(1) $L_H = 2.32 + 0.126\,t - 1.72\,Q_2 - 102\,Q_3 + 2.32\,Q_4$ (0.887) (0.0294) (0.721) (0.721) (0.697) $\hat{R} = 0.827$ $\hat{S} = 1.27$	(1) $G = 327 + 11.1\,t - 369\,Q_2 - 243\,Q_3 + 10.5\,Q_4$ (56.2) (1.97) (48.4) (48.4) (46.8) $\hat{R} = 0.927$ $\hat{S} = 85.3$
(2) $M_W = 0.741 + 0.0162\,t + 0.0247\,Q_2 - 0.0214\,Q_3 + 0.0667\,Q_4$ (0.0240) (0.000845) (0.0207) (0.0207) (0.0200) $\hat{R} = 0.969$ S $= 0.0365$	(2) L_H (3) M_W } common to I (4) SD_3
(3) $G_{IF} = 94.3 + 6.60\,t - 85.8\,Q_2 - 58.6\,Q_3 - 37.5\,Q_4$ (19.6) (7.690) (16.9) (16.9) (16.3) $\hat{R} = 0.912$ $\hat{S} = 29.8$	
(4) $SD^3 = 174 + 0.135\,t - 258\,Q_2 - 304\,Q^3 + 15.5\,Q_4$ (84.5) (2.97) (72.8) (72.8) (70.4) $\hat{R} = 0.749$ $\hat{S} = 128$	(5) $SD_4 = 273 + 11.3\,t - 72.7\,Q_2 - 49.7\,Q_3 - 18.9\,Q_4$ (20.0) (0.704) (17.3) (17.2) (16.7) $\hat{R} = 0.959$ $\hat{S} = 30.4$
(5) $T_R = 48.7 + 2.05\,t - 6.70\,Q_2 + 0.0449\,Q_3 + 8.31\,Q_4$ (6.89) (0.242) (5.94) (5.94) (5.74) $\hat{R} = 0.871$ $\hat{S} = 10.5$	(6) $T^* = 124 + 5.35\,t - 24.7\,Q_2 - 18.7\,Q_3 - 3.31\,Q_4$ (8.14) (0.286) (7.02) (7.01) (6.78) $\hat{R} = 0.968$ $\hat{S} = 12.4$
	(7) $T_C = 10.6 + 3.29\,t + 16.2\,Q_2 - 7.20\,Q_3 + 16.9\,Q_4$ (9.00) (0.316) (7.76) (7.75) (7.49) $\hat{R} = 0.908$ $\hat{S} = 13.7$

$$SD_3 = (T_G + D_G + e)$$

$$SD_4 = (T^* + T_P + T_C + H + T_G + D_G + e - T_R)$$

EDITORIAL NOTE

This remarkable paper, published at a time when careful statistical analysis of medium scale systems by advanced computational methods was in its infancy, is of interest for its scholarly econometric content. It was done in an environment of less than full recovery from war and drafted in English by a person whose native tongue was Japanese. It was published in English in a German economics journal. It is not surprising that it contained many sentences, phrases, or words that sound awkward in English.

This article is being reproduced exactly as it appeared in October, 1966, in *Zeitschrift für die gesamte Staatswissenschaft*, known since 1986 as *Journal of Institutional and Theoretical Economics/Zeitschrift für die gesamte Staatswissenschaft.* It is being reproduced with the kind permission of the editor, Professor Dr. h. c Rudolf Richter, and the publisher J. C. B. Mohr (Paul Siebeck).

I have noted on an Errata page, some changes that need to be made in order to convey a precise meaning or correct econometric interpretation. I have allowed some unusual phrases in English to stand unaltered as long as the reader can tell the meaning of what is being stated. In this way, we can see Kei Mori's own interpretation or analysis and also reproduce exactly what has been agreed to by the editor and publisher.

Lawrence R. Klein

ERRATA

		Change	To
p. 646	fn. *, l.3 from bottom	Uchiad	Uchida
p. 647	l. 21	feed	fed
p. 649	eqn. (2.2)	Ydt	Y_{dt}
p. 650	fn. 1	R.C. Liu	T.C. Liu
p. 652	eqn. (2.17)	W_t'	W_t
p. 653	l. 3	analoginizing	comparing
p. 653	l. 27	mixted	mixed
p. 653	l. 34	Z_t	z_t
p. 653	fn. 2	Z, Z_t	z, z_t
p. 654	l. 8	Z_t	z_t
p. 654	l. 19	parenthesis	parentheses
p. 655	Table 3.1	T_v	T_p
p. 659	Fig. 3.1	by Model Estimated	Model Estimated by
p. 663	l. 16 from bottom	k_2	K_2
p. 663	eqn. (11)	a_{kl}	a_{k_1}
p. 663	l. 14 from bottom	sustituted	substituted
p. 665	l. 1	effectuate	have

p. 665	l. 14	intrinsicly	intrinsically
p. 666	l. 7	$\bar{i}_t - 1$	$\bar{i}_{t-1}$
p. 666	l. 10, 11, 17, 20, 24	equation equations	expression expressions
p. 666	fn 2	scalers forcussing	scalars focussing
p. 668	l. 16	as is	is as
p. 669	l. 10 eqn. (18.C)	initially $D\{\bar{i}_{t-1}\} = \bar{a}_{21}$	initial $D\{\bar{i}_{t-1}) - \bar{a}_{21}$
p. 670	l. 26	P_2	p_2
p. 671	Table 4.1	laeding	leading
p. 681	A–2, l. 3	first quarter of 1955	first quarter of 1961
p. 682	l. 6	$d = 11.8$	$d = 1.18$

www.ingramcontent.com/pod-product-compliance
Lightning Source LLC
La Vergne TN
LVHW051054210926
848486LV00002B/111